Teresita

WILLIAM CURRY HOLDEN

Teresita

ILLUSTRATED BY
JOSÉ CISNEROS

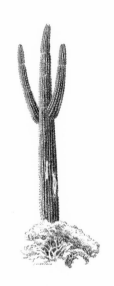

1978

Stemmer
House
PUBLISHERS, INC.
OWINGS MILLS, MARYLAND

Inquiries should be directed to
Stemmer House Publishers, Inc.
2627 Caves Road
Owings Mills, Maryland 21117

Published simultaneously in Canada by George J. McLeod, Limited, Toronto

A Barbara Holdridge book
Printed and bound in the United States of America
First Edition

Library of Congress Cataloging in Publication Data
Holden, William Curry, 1896–
    Teresita.
    "A Barbara Holdridge book."
    Bibliography: p. 235
    1. Urrea, Teresa.   2. Healers—Mexico—Biography.
3. Psychical research—Biography.
BF1283.U77H64   1978   972.08'1'0924   [B]   78-2321
ISBN 0-916144-24-0
ISBN 0-916144-25-9 pbk.

Contents

Illustrations

Acknowledgments

OF THOSE who have had a part in producing this account of the life of Teresa Urrea, I am indebted most of all to my wife, Frances. She has been part and parcel of the project from its outset in 1952. As companion, counselor, critic, interrogator, notetaker and reader of every paragraph of each of the several drafts of this book, she has added immeasurably to the interpretation of the character and role of Teresita.

Next, my gratitude goes to Elizabeth Fagg Olds for the professional assistance she has given without stint as to content, treatment and, above all, for her perceptive editing.

To Robert (Bob) Raviez, my able interpreter and field investigator, I am indebted for the "discovery" of Teresita.

For reading the manuscript and giving their valuable opinions I am grateful to Dr. Evelyn Montgomery, Dr. Jane Holden Kelley, Robert Green, Isabelle Hamilton Howe and Roger Pat Mayhugh.

To artists Peter Hurd and Manuel Acosta, both fluently bilingual, our appreciation for acting as interpreters on several pleasant expeditions to northern Mexico.

I am indebted to Victor D. Valadez for extensive translations and to Henry Estrello for expertly rendering into English many printed and manuscript sources.

For maps and drawings I am deeply obligated to Patricia Allgood and José Cisneros.

I am above all grateful to all those who furnished information by interview or letter: Manuel Acosta, Eduardo Aguirre, Gabriel Aguirre, Henry Aguirre, Mary Aguirre, Hardee Allen, Alberto L. Almado, Antonio Alvarado, Marcus Alvarado, Franco Alvarez, Sarah Micelena Anaya, A. A. Anderson, Magdalena Van Order Anderson, Josefina Soto de Armenta, Maria Santini de Barcenas, Russell Bean, Bandelio Bovadilla, Arcadia Bandini Brennan, Mrs. L. A. Burtch, Cleofos Calleros, Gilbert A. Cam, Maria Castella, José Angel Conobbio, George Dunning, Rebecca Trevino Duty, José Esquerres, Rita Faudoa, Erma Fergusson, Marieta Urrea Flores, Jennie Freeze, Joaquin Fregoso, Joyce Glass de Fregoso, Rachel French, George Gamble, Lena Garcia, Tomasita Garcia, W. E. Glenhill, Apolonaria Guitierrez, Marshall Hail, José S. Healy, Rafael Holquin, Peter Hurd, T. Lee, Celso Leon, Chester M. Lewis, Mrs. Irving Marshall, M. Martinez, J. H. McNeely, Ventura Mejia, Procopio Montoya, John H. Morrison, K. Murra, Solidad Newman, Luce Norte, Doyce B. Nunnis, Manuel Ortez, Ana Bequi de Packman, Luz Palomares, Rafael Palomares, Sr. and Sra Rudolfo Palomares, Abba Potter, Frank B. Putman, L. J. Rasmissen, J. B. Rhodes, Peter Rilley, José Rojo of Clifton, Arizona, José Rojo of Navojoa, Sonora, Margarita Royball, F. G. Salazar, Laura Van Order de Salazar, Solidad Salazar, Franco Samuels, Longina Sanchez, Angel Santini, Gustavo Santini, Peggy Carl Schlotzhauer, Marshall Sidebottom, Garnette Smith, Elizabeth Stein, Rose C. Stewart, Harriet Sweeting, J. B. Tomkins, Emilia Gutierrez de Torres, Anita Urrea de Trevino, Arthur Trevino, Antonio Urrea, Francisco Urrea, Goya Urrea, Rafael Urrea, Terry Urrea, Barger Vadette, José C. Valadez, Mrs. Harry Van Order, Harry Van Order, Katherine Wagner, Mrs. E. E. Wheeler, R. B. Willson and any others I may have overlooked inadvertently.

Introduction

I FIRST HEARD of the mysterious Saint of Cabora in 1951, from the Palomares family in the border town of Reynosa, Tamaulipas, near the east coast of Mexico. The following year I encountered her legend again while working with the Yaqui Indians in Sonora, on the west coast of Mexico. Later I found she was also a legend in Mexico City and in all of northern Mexico. The more I learned, the more fascinated I became with her amazing story.

Her star had risen quickly in the last decade of the nineteenth century, had passed rapidly and brilliantly across the sky of northern Mexico, and had set suddenly. Contemporary Mexican historians call her the Mexican Joan of Arc. The ranch of Cabora in northern Mexico, where she lived and practiced her healing arts, became for a time the Lourdes of Mexico. Although she never owned a weapon or led an army, she unwittingly inspired hundreds of brave men and women to go to their deaths shouting, "Long live the Saint of Cabora!" She possessed extraordinary psychic abilities and powers rarely heard of at the time. She cured tens of thousands of people of real or imaginary ills without remuneration of any kind, modestly contending that her gifts were God-given to help the afflicted. The title of "saint,"

which she never accepted, was not conferred on her by any ecclesiastical authority, but by hundreds of thousands of Mexicans
and Indians who loved and adored her. She was expelled from
Mexico at the age of nineteen because a dictator considered her
popularity with the masses a political threat to his regime. This
fascinating girl first intrigued and gradually became an obsession
with me. With my wife, Frances Mayhugh Holden, a professional
historical researcher, I took up her ephemeral trail and followed
it on every possible occasion for twenty-five years. Now I am ready
to tell her story.

In December of 1952 I was in the Yaqui Indian villages
located on the Río Yaqui southeast of Guaymas, Sonora. With
me as interpreter was Bob Raviez, a graduate student of anthro-
pology from Harvard University. Bob, who was born and reared
in San Antonio, Texas, was fluent in Spanish. He was gifted with
an aptitude for languages, and after spending a few weeks in the
Yaqui villages he had picked up enough Yaqui words to understand what the Indians were saying when talking among themselves. (Most Yaqui women speak only Yaqui. Many of the men
speak Spanish, some of them fluently.) Bob kept overhearing
references to La Santa de Cabora. But when he inquired who this
Santa might be, he found that the women would say nothing.
With the men he got nowhere either—only a word or two and a
shrug of the shoulders, suggesting that revealing information
about the Santa was in the same category of unacceptable behavior as disclosing intimate details about their own private lives,
a subject about which most Yaquis evidence a tight-lipped Vic-
torian prudery. We gave up attempting to solicit information from
the Yaquis concerning the Santa, and decided to make discreet
inquiries among descendants of the old Spanish families. This
was a group we had avoided since our first contact with the Yaquis
in 1934. The Yaquis from time immemorial had been, and still
were, enemies of all non-Yaquis except those of the Cahita lin-
guistic group of which they were members. The antagonism extended to the pure Spanish as well as to mestizos (of mixed

blood). Whatever government was in control of Mexico, they were against it. To be seen fraternizing with non-Yaquis would have caused the Indians to "clam up," and that would have ended our ethnological investigations.

One day we went to the primitive but fast-growing city of Obregón for supplies. In the market we saw an attractive, well-dressed and genteel woman who appeared to be in her sixties; her speech and manners indicated an aristocratic background. Observing that no Yaquis were in sight, Bob introduced us to the woman, explaining who we were and what we were doing. She acknowledged us with dignified reserve. Bob inquired if she might be a member of one of the old families from the West Coast. She replied that she belonged to the Palomares family of Alamos. When Bob told her of our relationship with the Palomares family of Reynosa, she became friendly and informative. Her name was Luz Palomares. We asked about the Saint of Cabora, and she revealed that she knew a great deal about her. We could tell from her enthusiastic response that she thought highly of La Santa, whose name, she said, was Teresa Urrea. She had belonged to the Urrea family, and all the old families had always called the girl Teresita, a diminutive and endearing term.

Señora Palomares told us that the best account of Teresa Urrea's life had been published in *La Opinión*, a Spanish newspaper published in Los Angeles in 1937. She still had one of the articles at her home in Hermosillo and said that if we would stop by on our way back to Texas she would give it to us.

Standing among the vegetable stalls in the market, she gave us a provocative sketch of Teresita. She was the natural daughter of Don Tomás Urrea and an Indian girl. She possessed "God-given powers" for curing all kinds of illnesses. People had flocked to Cabora by the thousands from all parts of Mexico in an immense wave of mass hysteria created by the "miracles" she had been seen to perform. Porfirio Díaz, alarmed that some of his political enemies might exploit this emotional upheaval and overthrow his dictatorship, had sent a full battalion of the Mexican army to arrest Teresita and conduct her to the international border at Nogales. He had forbade her to return under the penalty of being shot. All this had happened in 1892, before Señora Luz was born.

We asked her if she had seen pictures of La Santa. She said there were many pictures of her scattered about and that Teresita was a lovely, even beautiful, girl.

This accidental meeting with Señora Luz Palomares started a new quest. Later we did stop by her home in Hermosillo, and she brought out a copy of *La Opinión*, already yellowed with age. The article in question had appeared on February 28, 1937, in a feature section of eight pages, and was the first in a series of twelve about Teresa Urrea, written by an eminent Mexican historian, José C. Valades, and scheduled to appear weekly in special editions of the newspaper. A banner headline one-and-one-half inches high ran completely across the front page of this issue: "La Santa de Cabora." Beneath blazed another headline in red ink, three-quarters of an inch high, that said, when translated into English, "The First Miraculous Cures." Also on the front page was an eight-by-ten-inch picture of Teresa shown curing a peasant woman's baby. The subject of this extended journalistic treatment had died over thirty years earlier.

Much later we learned that this picture was a typical view of Teresita after she was seventeen years old: constantly surrounded by people everywhere she went.

Valades was a superb writer, graphic, fast-paced and objective. His account intensified our desire to pursue the story of La Santa.

Her trail has lured us from coast to coast in the United States, from Houston to Los Angeles, by way of San Antonio and El Paso in Texas and, in Arizona, through Nogales, Safford, Thatcher, Solomonville and Clifton, thence to St. Louis and New York. We traversed Mexico several times from Reynosa in Tamaulipas, by way of Mexico City to Sinaloa de Leyna and Ocoroni in the state of Sinaloa, to Alamos, Navojoa, Obregón, the ranch of Cabora, Guaymas, Hermosillo and Nogales in the state of Sonora.

Our first major trip was to California, for we hoped to find in Los Angeles the newspaper files of *La Opinión* containing the eleven other chapters by Valades about La Santa de Cabora. We were elated to discover that *La Opinión* was listed in the Los Angeles Yellow Pages. But when we arrived at the address, we were told that a fire in the 1940s had destroyed the original plant and all the newspaper files. However, the editor, noticing our dismay, hastened to assure us that all was not lost. He recalled Valades's articles and explained that since 1913 his publishing company had maintained a sister Spanish-language newspaper called *La Prensa* in San Antonio, Texas. The feature section containing the articles on Teresa Urrea had been run concurrently in both newspapers.

Returning to San Antonio, we found *La Prensa* in the upstairs of an old two-story building facing the market, part of the original business center of the city. The building had been mellowed by time, mold and dust, but the complete files, adequately bound, were intact. The staff, with the courtesy typical of Spanish-American culture, brought out the volume for 1937. We had brought with us our portable photostatic equipment, something new at the time and a rather heavy, bulky and clumsy affair. We hauled it up the narrow stairs to photostat the eleven articles we did not have. Later the articles were translated from Spanish into English.

Although painstakingly researched by Valades, the articles dealt only with certain dramatic incidents and episodes during the eighteenth and nineteenth years of Teresita's life. Little or nothing was related about her family, childhood, extrasensory powers, the important part she unintentionally and innocently played in the inception of the Mexican Revolution, and the last thirteen years of her life.

In time we visited more than a hundred relatives and friends of the Urrea family in Texas, Arizona, California, Sonora and

Sinaloa. From them we obtained information that we recorded in copious notes and many hours of tape recordings. My wife was a superb interrogator (and, incidentally, an excellent camp cook). Most of the relatives had some documentary materials: letters, photographs, legal papers, newspaper clippings and other printed matter. From these sources I have put together an account of the immediate family of Teresa Urrea and of her career. I am aware of the numerous questions raised by the narrative that follows, but I have done the best I could with the sources available to me.

My approach has been that of a historian. I have faithfully tried to report how Teresita's extrasensory powers were demonstrated, but I do not feel qualified to explain them. It is my hope that this account will interest professional researchers of the occult, who may be better able to understand this gifted and highly complex young woman.

I have often been asked why we found this relatively unknown historical figure from a remote and obscure region so exciting and irresistible. The answer is not easy. Something about her dedication and devotion to the afflicted and the oppressed, her fragile beauty, her extrasensory powers and her radiant influence, which transcended distances, religious creeds and political systems, all reveal an arresting personality and an exceptional individual. In a benign and provocative way, her hypnotic spell lives on.

Lubbock, Texas   W.C.H.
March 1978

The Principals

Lauro Aguirre, engineer, scholar and devoted friend of Teresita and Don Tomás

Antonio Alvarado, natural son of Don Tomás and Juliana Alvarado

Marcos Alvarado, brother of Juliana Alvarado

Gabriela Cantúa, mistress of Don Tomás

Cayetana Chávez, mother of Teresita

Cruz Chávez, leader and martyr of Tomochic

Porfirio Díaz, president and later dictator of Mexico

Josefina Félix, friend and companion of Teresita

Marieta Urrea Flores, daughter of Don Tomás and Gabriela Cantúa

Manuel Gustélum, priest at Uruachi and defamer of Teresita

Apolonaria Urrea Gutiérrez, daughter of Don Tomás by Doña Loreto

Huila, herb doctor and housekeeper of the Cabora Ranch

Anita Urrea Treviño, daughter of Don Tomás and Gabriela Cantúa

Apolonaria Ortiz Urrea, mother of Don Tomás

Buenaventura Urrea, natural son of Don Tomás and a girl named Celena

Doña Loreto Urrea, wife of Don Tomás

Don Miguel Urrea, uncle and patron of Don Tomás
Teresa Urrea, born Niña Garcia Nona Maria Rebecca Chávez,
    called Teresita
Don Tomás Urrea, father of Teresita

Teresita

Prologue

On the morning of September 5, 1891, a young reporter of Latin descent, notebook in hand, faced his harassed editor across a wide expanse of cluttered desk.

"I have an assignment for you, Mendoza," the rough-voiced, gray-haired chief of the *Arizona Daily Star* shouted above the roar of the press. He gestured with the stem of his pipe to a rickety chair beside the desk, and the young man sat down.

Mopping the perspiration from his face with a dirty towel and running his fingers through a mass of unruly hair, the editor continued.

"There is some excitement down in Sonora at a ranch called Cabora. A young girl there is attracting widespread interest as a healer, and some reports say that she performs miracles. The people there—the *gente*—call her a saint, La Santa de Cabora. I want you to go down there and learn the truth about her. Have you heard of her?"

"Yes, sir. There is much talk. They say the crowds flocking to the ranch number in the thousands."

"Do you believe in miracles?" the older man inquired pointedly.

"No."

"Good. If you did, you would not be the man for this assignment."

"Why send me?" Mendoza shifted uneasily in his seat, uncomfortable at the prospect of a long, arduous journey.

"Because I want the truth about this girl. Of all my reporters, I think you are the least likely to be taken in by pretense or quackery. I have had some inquiries about her from the Los Angeles and San Francisco papers, and I want you to bring back an honest report. Get an interview with her and observe what she does."

"Very well, sir. How do I make the trip?"

"The Sud Pacifico, as you know, has been completed to Hermosillo. You can get that far by train. There you can rent a horse for the remainder of the journey. You can get provisions at the ranches and army garrisons along the way."

Four weeks later, Mendoza again entered the editor's office, triumphantly brandishing a sheaf of foolscap.

"Here is your story, sir, 'La Niña de Cabora' as I found her," he shouted over the din of the machinery. "The Pacific Coast papers may be interested in what I saw."

Before glancing at the copy, the editor said, "Did you actually interview the girl?"

"Yes."

"Who is she?"

"Her name is Teresa Urrea. She is the illegitimate daughter of Don Tomás Urrea. The family call her Teresita. To the *gente* she is the Saint of Cabora."

The editor looked at the manuscript. "Why the caption, 'La Niña de Cabora'?"

"It is the familiar and endearing term. To me, it seems more appropriate."

The older man avidly read through the last few paragraphs of the long, yellow pages, then looked hard and long at his young protegé. "She didn't convert you, did she, Mendoza?"

"No, sir. The fact is, she didn't even try. She makes no pretense of being a saint."

"But her cures, are they miracles?"

"That I do not know. I saw some strange things I cannot explain. Neither can she."

"I must say, Mendoza, if she did not convert you, she did make a profound impression on you."

"She did indeed. She is a beautiful, sincere, dedicated young woman—not a faker by any means. What she does is genuine. I confess I do not understand some of her cures—even though I saw her perform them with my own eyes."

Chapter One

THE CIRCUMSTANCES OF Teresita's birth were neither extraordinary nor promising. The natural daughter of Don Tomás Urrea,
a grandee of distinguished lineage, and Cayetana Chávez, a
fifteen-year-old Tehueco Indian girl, Teresita seemed a most
unlikely candidate for miracle-worker. Her parents could hardly
have been more disparate, and, although brief couplings of the
aristocracy and native Indians were common enough, the offspring of such unions could expect to suffer the rejection of one
or both parents. Fortunately for Teresa Urrea, she was eventually
to gain the proud recognition and support of her powerful father.

The name Urrea is said to be a Moorish corruption of the
Spanish word for gold. The original Urreas were Christian
Moors in Spain. After centuries of intermarriage, the Urreas
appeared more Spanish than many Spaniards. Some of the later
descendants had a fair complexion, light hair and green eyes—
physical characteristics that may have been introduced when the
Visigoths invaded Spain in the fifth and sixth centuries.

The Urreas of Spain produced several churchmen, four
bishops and a cardinal, but those who migrated to Mexico
turned their attention to secular matters. The New World
branch of the family included two governors, a general, several
mine owners, a number of *hacendados* (a combination of cattle-

men and planters), and several who devoted themselves to politics and law. One of Don Tomás's ancestors, Lieutenant Manuel Urrea, had helped found Culiacán, the oldest Spanish settlement in northwest Mexico.

Tomás's father died soon after the boy's birth, leaving the child in the care of his strong-willed mother, Apolonaria Ortiz Urrea. The task of raising a small boy was shared with her late husband's brother, Miguel, a wealthy landowner handsomely supported by two profitable mines, sprawling ranches in Sonora and Sinaloa, and other lucrative assets. Miguel and his wife were childless, and young Tomás soon became their favorite nephew, as generously indulged as an only child. When the boy was old enough Miguel proposed sending him to Germany for an education, but the headstrong youth had other plans, as his uncle soon discovered.

Tall and strikingly handsome, with light skin and auburn hair, Tomás was happiest astride a spirited horse and silver-studded saddle. He cut a splendid figure as the dashing cavalier with a *pistola* on either hip, the envy of all the boys and adored hero of the girls at Sinaloa Leyna. The way of life at his uncle's nearby hacienda suited his romantic temperament, as did the many gallant adventures with the daughters of the vaqueros on the ranch. At the prospect of school in a faraway country, Tomás protested so violently that Don Miguel abandoned all plans for his nephew's European education. But there were still other matters to be settled. The young man would soon be ready for the responsibilities of a family.

Marriages in upper-class Spanish families were carefully arranged by the parents of both the bride and groom, with due regard to social position, wealth, religion and politics. Such a system guaranteed purity in the legitimate blood lines. Don Miguel skillfully plotted a marriage between Tomás and his niece Loreto, the only child of his sister, Micaela Urrea de Eseberri. After the wedding of Tomás and his cousin, Don

J. CISNEROS

Miguel made the young man manager of the ranch of Santana, a vast holding extending many leagues north of the town of Ocoroni, Sinaloa.

Marriage brought considerable stability and order into Don Tomás's life. He supervised the ranch with energy and skill, and observed the amenities expected of him in his relations with Doña Loreto. In time, ten children were born, seven of whom lived to maturity. Esteemed as able, honest and sober, Don Tomás was a model citizen in all but one respect: he had a roving eye and a weakness for young women. While still young, Tomás had a short-lived affair with a girl named Celena (no one could ever remember her last name), and the result was a boy child, Buenaventura, older than any of his legitimate children. Later Don Tomás acknowledged him, granted the boy the Urrea name, and arranged to have him reared in Doña Loreto's household.

After the birth of Doña Loreto's third child, Don Tomás's restless gaze fastened on Cayetana, the fourteen-year-old daughter of a vaquero. The child of this tall, slender young girl and her impetuous overlord was christened Niña Garcia Nona Maria Rebecca Chávez. Just when her name became simply Teresa is not known. The child was born October 15, 1873, on the dirt floor of a ramada, or brush arbor, on the bank of an arroyo—a gully or dry creek—half a mile from the headquarters of the Santana ranch.

Three years after the birth of Teresa, and after two more children had been born to Doña Loreto, Don Tomás was attracted to a small and shapely Indian girl, Juliana Alvarado; and in due time a boy, Antonio Alvarado, appeared in another ramada on the ranch. Don Tomás never publicly acknowledged Antonio; but he knew who he was and kept a close watch on the boy, giving him responsible jobs on the ranches. Through hard work and loyalty to his father, Antonio eventually became a wealthy and respected man. Just where the eye of Don Tomás traveled between Buenaventura and Teresita, between Teresita and Antonio, and after Antonio, is open to speculation; but, by all accounts, this was a vigorous and virile period in his life.

No one knows when Don Tomás first became aware that Teresita was his child. Mother and daughter lived with Cayetana's oldest sister, a domineering woman burdened with a brood of her own. Certainly a light-colored baby among a collection of brown children was food for gossip. Most of the vaqueros and their women could easily guess the identity of Teresita's father, and soon the browbeating sister hounded the truth out of Cayetana. As was her habit before Teresa's birth, Cayetana's sister continued to treat the young mother as one of her own: ordering, demanding, bullying, scolding. Her henpecked husband resented Cayetana, especially after the girl produced this new mouth to feed.

As Teresita crawled on the dirt floor of her aunt's ramada, and later began to walk, her Spanish traits became even more conspicuous. Her large eyes, set far apart, changed to brown, strikingly different from the inky black eyes of the vaqueros' children. Her hair became auburn and slightly wavy. With her light skin, dark red hair and brown eyes, Teresita offered a distinct contrast to the flock of brown-skinned, black-haired offspring of the ranch hands. The girl's incongruous appearance fanned the hostility of her aunt toward the "bastard child of *el patrón*." Easily intimidated by the older woman, Cayetana got nowhere in her efforts to defend her child.

In spite of her aunt's tongue-lashings and occasional cuff on the bottom, Teresita's childhood was happy and carefree. Strong, healthy and lithe, she ran, climbed, scuffled and competed with the best of the others. Teresita wore no clothes until she began to walk, and then the girl's dress consisted of a single garment of coarse material that reached to her ankles. Her young boy cousins wore nothing until they were three or four, at which age they were put into knee-length, homespun shifts. This type of garment served them until adolescence, when they were given trousers.

Teresita

When Teresita was three, her aunt moved her family, including Cayetana and her daughter, from the ramada on the arroyo to Protero, a compound, or village, consisting of some thirty ramadas for the workers at the headquarters of the Santana ranch. Here there were scores of children to romp with. One of their favorite sports was riding burros, of which the ranch had a sizable number. By nature, burros are docile and seldom vicious, and the gentlest of these patient beasts were given to the children. Often four or five boys would climb on the back of one burro, forcing the hindmost rider off the burro's rump. The ousted boy would then run alongside and jump to the front, claiming the seat of honor and pushing the last player to the ground in a rotational "king of the mountain" game atop the patient, slow-moving animal's back.

Little girls at the time were trained from earliest childhood not to participate in the boys' rough sports, only to watch and admire. But Teresita scorned the passive role assigned her. Soon she began to join the young hellions, easily surpassing them at their own games. Her adventurous nature, sunny disposition and childish beauty made her a favorite of the vaqueros, who often lifted the laughing child astride their horses and let her ride in front.

Gradually Teresita's auburn waves changed to a darker brown, her eyes became more luminous, and her voice grew soft and melodious. By the time she was seven she was a beguiling child, loved and petted by most of the working people on the ranch. Only her aunt remained untouched by the child's beauty, and, like the fabled wicked step-sister, continued to treat Teresita with hostility and scorn.

Not that Teresita was angelic. On the contrary, she was mischievous and cunning, the instigator of more pranks than any other child in the village. When caught and confronted by her elders, she turned on her charm in such a disarming fashion that she usually got off scot-free while the less resourceful children were severely reprimanded.

By the time Teresita turned seven, Doña Loreto's household contained four children of her own, two boys and two girls, in addition to Don Tomás's natural son, Buenaventura. The girls remained aloof, and Teresita saw them only when they came and went with their mother in a handsome carriage. The three boys, however, often played with the children of the vaqueros. Teresita led a friendly, rough-and-tumble existence with her legitimate half-brothers, though no mention was ever made of their blood relationship.

Had politics and the national election of 1880 not interrupted the happy idyll, the good life at Santana might have continued, and the dramatic events that later occurred at the ranch of Cabora might have taken place in Sinaloa instead of Sonora.

In 1876 General Porfirio Díaz rebelled against Sebastián Lerdo de Tejada, recently elected to a second term as president of Mexico. Supported by loyal henchmen, Díaz organized an armed rebellion, setting forth the Plan of Tuxtepec. The central issue of the Plan guaranteed "effective suffrage and no reelection," thus forbidding more than one term per president. The insurrection gathered momentum like a prairie fire on a windy day, sweeping the scholarly Lerdo from office. The national congress promptly elected Díaz president. Four years later, Díaz, ignoring the promises of his original campaign, presented himself again for the presidency. Lerdo, resurrecting the "no reelection" slogan with which Díaz had ousted him in 1876, announced his own candidacy. By this time, however, Díaz had so effectively consolidated his forces—expelling his enemies and installing supporters at all levels of government—that Lerdo did not stand a chance. Although a semblance of constitutionality was observed in the 1880 elections for governor, the wily Díaz made sure that his hand-picked choices were installed in every state.

In Sinaloa, the Díaz candidate was Gabriel Leyna, and the Lerdo contender Miguel Castelo. Don Tomás, a long-time supporter of Lerdo, took an active part in the campaign by Castelo, who won the election and was installed as governor. His victory was brief. Díaz, claiming foul play, declared the election void and ordered his army commandant in Sinaloa to arrest Castelo and proclaim Gabriel Leyna governor. Castelo was banished from the country on pain of death if he ever returned. The puppet governor began retaliations against the leaders of Lerdo's party, and Don Tomás learned he was a marked man. He was faced with two alternatives: he could go to the governor, hat in hand, beg forgiveness and swear loyalty to the Díaz regime, or he could remove himself from the state. Don Tomás was no turncoat. He chose the latter course of action.

Chapter Two

BEFORE LEAVING SINALOA, Don Tomás prudently discussed his situation with his uncle Miguel. Equally alarmed by the scare tactics of Díaz, the older man advised his nephew to depart as soon as possible, offering him three generous options. The first two were to take charge of his uncle's mines or to manage Miguel's business property at Alamos in Sonora. The third alternative was to move to the ranch of Cabora, also in Sonora. This last was of much greater interest. Mining and business held little appeal for Don Tomás; his life was in ranching. The Cabora ranch had been a wedding present from Miguel to Tomás and Loreto, and from there he could manage three of Miguel's nearby ranches: Las Vacas, Aquihuiquichi ("the place of the little cactus flower" in Mayo dialect), and Santa María.

Don Tomás planned his departure with great care, entrusting the management of the Santana ranch in Sinaloa to his Ortiz cousins. From previous visits to the Sonora ranches, he knew they were poorly developed, understocked and undermanned. With Don Miguel's approval, Tomás chose his retainers and household goods, selecting as well some forty of the best bulls at Santana, sixty horses and a herd of burros. A dozen steers and a flock of goats were brought along to feed the growing caravan on the trail. He scoured the countryside for oxcarts to carry the household goods of Doña Loreto and the scant belongings of the families of the retainers. Doña Loreto was fond of honey, and the cargo included several hives of bees—the first, it is said, to be introduced into Sonora.

The departure from Sinaloa in the late fall of 1880 was not unlike the biblical exodus of Abraham and Lot with their wives and concubines, their maidservants and manservants, their flocks and their herds. Among the retainers were Antonio Alvarado, then three years old, and his mother, Juliana; Cayetana Chávez and her daughter, Teresita, age seven; and Cayetana's older sister and her family. All together, over a hundred people filled the train of oxcarts. Drawn by patient, plodding oxen, the carts were loaded to the rims with furniture, supplies and utensils, the women and children perched precariously on top. Doña Loreto and those of her children too young to ride horseback traveled in a comfortable carriage. Entranced by the whole spectacle, Teresita and Antonio Alvarado kept pace on shaggy burros.

Covering about ten miles a day, the caravan headed north to El Fuerte, then stopped for twenty-four hours to ferry the many carts across the Río Fuerte. From there it kept to the left of the foothills of the Sierra Madre to the Río Navojoa, again crossed by ferry raft. Another three days brought the travelsore party to Cabora, approximately one hundred miles southeast of Guaymas and thirty-five miles northwest of Alamos.

Just short of the headquarters at Cabora, however, the weary leader abruptly stopped, appalled by the disastrous sight that met his eyes. The place had obviously been raided by Yaqui Indians, and was a shambles: ramadas had been burned to the ground, the corrals were wrecked, not a head of livestock was to be seen. Only the hand-dug well and water trough were spared. The travelers camped overnight while Don Tomás considered his next step.

His decision the next morning was to move on to Aquihui-quichi. There the facilities were better and the place could be

more easily defended. There he would establish the women and children and return with the vaqueros and workers to rebuild Cabora. At Aquihuiquichi, Tomás learned that the Cabora raid had occurred two weeks before, and that in addition to the property damage, the Yaquis had killed two vaqueros, carried off a woman and two children, rounded up and driven away the entire heard of horses—mares, colts, saddle horses and stallions—and taken an undetermined number of cattle for their useful hides. Aquihuiquichi, Santa María and Las Vacas had not been molested.

Don Tomás spent several days getting work crews organized at Cabora. Then he took Doña Loreto, her children and her personal servants to Alamos, where he installed them in one of Don Miguel's most pretentious houses, La Capilla (The Chapel), a spacious dwelling that greatly pleased both Loreto's pious nature and her love of the finer creature comforts. Later Don Tomás improved La Capilla further by adding rooms, servants' quarters, stables, and facilities for poultry, hogs and milk cows. At the time she first moved into the grand house, Loreto had four children of her own in addition to Buenaventura, whom her husband had adopted. During the twelve years of her residency there, Tomás visited often enough to give her six more, three of whom lived to maturity.

Returning to Aquihuiquichi, Don Tomás found that the vaqueros and workers he had brought from Santana had erected a whole new village of ramadas, all made from mesquite—posts, beams, even the brush on top. The sap had not yet dried in the posts, and leaves on the brush were still green. Walking from ramada to ramada, he greeted the women, patted the children and talked earnestly to the men. When Don Tomás reached the shelter of Teresita's aunt, the children regarded the *patrón* shyly and with utmost respect. He patted some of them gently on the head, including Teresita, whom he treated in the same affectionate but impersonal manner as her brown-skinned cousin, a girl about her own age.

Don Tomás assembled the vaqueros and workers, and with an oxcart full of hand tools and staples, they started for Cabora, driving the herd of horses brought from Santana. On arrival, the workers began building ramadas, while the vanqueros searched the surrounding country for Urrea cattle. Realizing that the work at Cabora would be hazardous, and possibly futile, unless he reached some understanding with the Mayo and Yaqui Indians, Don Tomás boldly determined to visit each village and confer with the leaders face to face. He set out through the rugged countryside for the Indian settlements, accompanied by Marcos Alvarado, one of his favorite retainers.

Several settlements of Mayos lived along Arroyo Cocoraqui, between Cabora and the Gulf of California. Don Tomás went to each of these, assembled the head men of the village, and explained his intention to reoccupy Cabora. He offered to give them work, treat them fairly, and from time to time donate cattle for their fiestas. In times of starvation, he would help to the best of his resources. Each negotiation was a slow, tedious process, as the Indians pondered, deliberated and debated. But Tomás patiently awaited their answers. And in the end, each village accepted the terms of the new *patrón* of Cabora.

Don Tomás then rode to the Yaqui villages, eight of them, along the Río Yaqui, about twenty miles to the north. In each village he repeated his offer, carefully avoiding any reference to the recent raid on Cabora. The Yaquis were more suspicious, reserved and obstinate in their dealings. He and Marcos had to listen to long, bitter diatribes against the Mexican government, the unscrupulous miners and greedy ranchers. Don Tomás agreed that the government had treated them shamefully, telling of his own opposition to the policies of Porfirio Díaz and describing his banishment from Sinaloa. These pronouncements softened the Yaquis' hostility; they listened to his proposals. In some villages, negotiations went on for as long as two or three days. Eventually, all agreed to respect Don Tomás's property.

Both the Mayo and Yaqui tribes kept their agreements.

Never again was Cabora raided. In the early years the peace was maintained as a result of Don Tomás's diplomacy; later Cabora was considered a holy place by both tribes. Don Tomás also kept his part of the agreement, employing a considerable number of Mayos and Yaquis on the ranches, especially at Cabora. They made good and dependable workers.

With the threat of Indian raids ended, Don Tomás turned his attention to developing the ranches, aided by large loans from his uncle. He became a demon for hard work, spending day after day in the saddle, supervising his construction crew with astonishing energy. The improvements at Cabora were made on the south side of Arroyo Cocoraqui, overlooking a steep bluff some twenty to twenty-five feet high. On the north side and farther down, the arroyo widened with a sloping north bank, leaving several hundred acres of comparatively level, rich land only a few feet above the watercourse. With low, diverting dams along the bed of the arroyo, this tract of land could be irrigated during the summer rainy season, while the arroyo flowed. Don Tomás employed a sizable crew of Indians to clear the land and then sent for Lauro Aguirre, an engineer he had known in Sinaloa, to supervise the building of the dams and to lay out irrigation ditches. When at last it was put into production, this plot of land yielded sufficient corn to feed the four hundred or more people on the four ranches. Scarcely a grain was lost as it was ground on metates and made into tortillas.

Don Tomás also gave great attention to improving the quality of cattle on the ranches. Native stock at the time—varicolored, rangy, with long legs, thin bodies and long sharp horns—appeared to be all hide, stringy muscles and bone. Yet, these cattle had hardihood and endurance that enabled them to survive droughts. Realizing that his problem was to introduce more meat and fat into this rugged breeding stock, he visited distant ranches looking for better bulls to supplement those he had brought from Sinaloa. Then he increased the size of his herds to the capacity of the pastures by retaining all those females not barren or too old or stringy, and by converting the steers into hides, tallow, soap and jerky. There was little market for steers on the hoof.

Every few months Don Tomás visited Alamos for several days, and faithfully fulfilled his obligations as husband, while he attended to business and supervised improvements at La Capilla. He made a special effort to be present for the birth of Doña Loreto's children, who arrived with absolute regularity, one each year. But although he appeared occasionally with Doña Loreto at social functions, she could never get him to church. During the long intervals between visits to his household at La Capilla, Tomás often enjoyed the bed and company of young women attached to his other establishments, leaving the problem of procurement to a loyal *peón de estribo*. This "servant of the stirrup," or groom, accompanied his *patrón* wherever he went, usually riding a few respectful paces behind. At one point Don Tomás considered making Marcos Alvarado his *péon de estribo*, but Marcos did not possess the necessary qualifications for such a delicate position. He was stolid, hardworking, dependable, a good judge of horses, cattle and men, but he was shy and silent with women, untutored in the diplomacy of the bedchamber. Don Tomás wisely put him in charge of the cattle on all the ranches.

Then Tomás found a man who was not worth his salt in the branding pen but was superb at anticipating his master's desire for women and discreetly arranging trysts. Cosimero was a young man of slight build and reasonably good looks, with a personable manner and persuasive tongue. Devotedly loyal to his master, he served Don Tomás until the *patrón* died, and then continued on as a member of the household until his own death.

Cosimero knew and understood Don Tomás, his weaknesses and virtues, perhaps better than any other person. He became indispensable to his master's day-to-day existence, attending to his horses, acting as valet when necessary, and carefully arranging nocturnal engagements. Although Tomás played the devoted husband when at Loreto's side, he abandoned the role during his long absences from Alamos, openly eyeing any fresh and promising girl—whether in town, Indian village, ramada, or on a path in the country. As always, Cosimero discreetly took charge of the details. According to one grandson, Don Tomás would give his servant a scarcely perceptible signal—a nod or a wink—and the *peón de estribo* would disappear, returning a short time later with the arrangements for a rendezvous. These encounters were usually brief, or at most for a day or two, but the young woman was always well remunerated.

Though his affairs were numerous, Don Tomás never let his private passions interfere with the steady management and improvement of his vast holdings. At Cabora, the culmination of his construction activities was represented by the Casa Grande. He had planned the house as a complete unit, but the task was so enormous that he built it in separate sections. The original design called for rock masonry with walls two feet thick, and that was how Don Tomás constructed the first unit, a massive room planned as the northwest corner of the house. Although the Yaquis had kept the peace, he could not be sure that some new indignity of the Díaz government would not touch off another outbreak. As a defense measure, Don Tomás built a circular stone watchtower, with loopholes in every direction, adjacent to the original room. A bedroom was added above, with a staircase entrance through the watchtower.

By the time this part of the house was finished, it was apparent that the quarrying, hauling and shaping of the stone for the remainder of the house would require many years. The *patrón* built the other additions to the Casa Grande of adobe on rock foundations, in a fraction of the time. The north wing was built near the edge of the cliff on the south side of Arroyo Cocoraqui. Seventy meters long and eight meters wide, the wing featured a luxury found only in the finest houses of the time: a room designed as a toilet, beneath which a tunnel permitted waste to be flushed out occasionally to the side of the cliff over the arroyo.

The next project entailed building another wing of equal

width and length, extending south from the original rock room, to form an L. The veranda on this extension was an arcade, its columns and arches of homemade fired brick. Then a parallel wing was constructed at the east end, forming a U with the open side on the south. No portal was built on the east unit. Across the open side on the south Don Tomás built a high picket fence of heavy posts set close together, completely enclosing an enormous patio. A heavy gate, wide enough for a carriage and surmounted by an impressive arch, formed the entranceway to the Casa Grande.

Beyond the great house were the ramadas of the vaqueros and workers, situated in three separate groups—one to the southwest of the Casa Grande and south of the arroyo, one across the arroyo to the northeast, and the third across the arroyo to the northwest. The two *mayordomos*, one in charge of vaqueros and the other of the farm workers, had separate adobe houses with verandas on either side.

Many of Don Tomás's construction workers stayed on as field hands, swelling the number to approximately forty-five altogether. An equal number of vaqueros worked together as a group, moving from one ranch to another during the roundups and branding of the Urrea livestock. Since most of the men had families, the ranches supported some four hundred people in all, most of them located at Cabora.

When Antonio Alvarado was eighty-five, in 1962, his recollections of the Casa Grande were still vivid. He had been there when the first stone was laid, he had witnessed the construction, he had lived there during the period of its affluence and notoriety, its gradual deterioration, and its ultimate collapse into a mound of rock, rubble and earth.

He remembered that the west wing of the Casa Grande had contained bedrooms, a chapel, the kitchen and the original large room, which remained Don Tomás's bedroom and library. *El patrón* was an avid reader and had many books. The portal in front of the west wing was the outdoor living and eating area. A long table, with benches on either side accommodating twenty or more people, was opposite the kitchen. The portal of the north wing, which had bedrooms and the toilet, was for shade and general use. The east wing was for storage and domestic industries—tannery, wood shop and blacksmith shop. Antonio well remembered the flower garden and the plum tree, for as a young man he had done his stint carrying water from the well for that tree and for the plants within the patio.

With the improvements completed, the *patrón* turned his driving energy to making the ranches more profitable, in order to repay Uncle Miguel the money lent to renovate Cabora. In addition to selling cattle on the hoof, for which there was small demand, he developed a subsidiary market for hides, tallow, soap and jerky. Cattle were butchered on the ranch and almost all parts of the animal were used. The meat was cut into thin strips, dried in the sun, and then stored in the warehouse where it would keep for months or until sold. A double tanning vat was built just east of the Casa Grande, and the hides were stored in the warehouse of the east wing. Some were made into saleable leather objects; others were sold in bulk to makers of saddles, harnesses, shoes, boots and other items. Tallow was rendered and converted into candles and soap, two of the most indispensable items in Mexico, even in the huts of the poorest natives. In all, Don Tomás created a diversified, self-sustaining ranching operation, a novelty for its time in northern Mexico.

During the early 1880s, Doña Loreto and her daughters made occasional visits to Cabora in their fine carriage, but stayed only a few days. In spite of the renovations underway at Cabora, Loreto was always eager to get back to La Capilla and the less strenuous life in Alamos. In choosing not to cater to her husband's constant sexual needs and desires, she was to cause herself great unhappiness in the years to come.

Returning from a routine visit to Alamos one day in 1885, Don Tomás and Cosimero stopped at a little ranch owned by a family named Cantúa. They dismounted and went inside to visit, sip coffee and pass the time of day. Their refreshments were served by a beautiful young girl in her middle teens, already fully developed and voluptuous, yet modest and respectful toward the family's guests. The girl's café-au-lait skin was smooth and soft, her hazel eyes large and sparkling. Don Tomás noted her shapely ankles and bare feet beneath the plain but carefully ironed dress. All this was too much for this experienced judge of women to ignore. For a moment he was appraisingly silent. Then, turning toward his host, Don Tomás exclaimed, "Ramón, where have you been keeping this lovely vision?"

Ramón Cantúa replied, "It so happens, señor, that every time you have been here she has been away visiting relatives."

"Then fortune is with me today!" He turned to the girl. "And how are you called?"

She dropped her eyes and in a low voice replied, "Gabriela."

"I should have known it had something to do with the angels!"

Gabriela discreetly studied this tall, outspoken stranger, a commanding man of middle years, fair-skinned, with light-brown eyes and a brown mustache. Don Tomás in turn could not take his eyes off the splendid young woman. He noted every contour, from head to foot, and was tremendously pleased. The coffee was forgotten. "Don Ramón," he said softly, "never let her visit her relatives again. I will be passing here often, and when I do, it would please me if she were here."

Ramón's answer could not be heard. But there was no doubt that the poor ranchero was overwhelmed by the rich *hacendado's* attentions to his daughter.

Neither the exact date of Gabriela's appearance at Cabora nor the details of the arrangements made with her parents are known, but within a few weeks the girl was permanently installed as the mistress of Cabora. When stories of the beautiful newcomer reached Alamos, Doña Loreto ordered her *mozo* to prepare her carriage and drive her to Cabora. Forewarned of his indignant wife's approach, Don Tomás met her carriage just outside the patio gate. Loreto made no move to get out of the carriage, and Don Tomás did not offer to assist her. They stared at one another in charged silence. Finally Doña Loreto timidly addressed her husband.

"Tomás, I have come to see about that woman."

Don Tomás went taut with anger and looked at her fiercely. "Loreto, you are never, not ever, to see me in Cabora! I will see you at Alamos!"

With that he caught the bridles and turned the carriage around, facing it in the direction from which it had come. Then he crossed to the driver's side and said brusquely, "Take the Señora back to Alamos!" Taking the buggywhip from its socket, he gave the horses a mighty lash and threw the whip back to the driver, shouting, "¡*Vamonos*! Get going!" The carriage lurched forward and sped down the slope at a gallop, ending Doña Loreto's last visit to Cabora.

Fiercely resenting the usurper, Loreto suffered mentally and physically. The dominance of the Church made divorce impossible; and even if such a thing had been permitted, the property settlement would have presented great difficulties, since she and Don Tomás were joint owners of Cabora. After the initial shock, however, Loreto's anger softened: the shared loaf was better than none. And somehow Tomás kept the peace between his separate households, for his wife's last four children were born during the same span of time as Gabriela's first four.

Following Gabriela's arrival at Cabora, Don Tomás's *peón de estribo* was not kept quite so busy. Tomás was now forty years of age, twenty-five years older than his young mistress, and *muy macho*—the chieftain of the ranch, the home, the wives, the children and all else. This role, however, was to be altered drastically during the last third of his life.

Chapter Three

A FEW MILES FROM CABORA, at the smaller ranch of Aquihuiquichi, Teresita grew up in a simple mesquite hut, surrounded
by the family of her shrewish aunt. Sometime before 1888, her
mother disappeared completely, perhaps provoked beyond endurance by her sister's scolding tongue. Possibly Cayetana
attached herself to the first vaquero or mine worker who promised
escape from Sonora. In any case, mother and daughter were not
to see each other again for many years.

A half-hearted student, more drawn to horses than to books,
Teresita went to school with her cousins and playmates. She was
an exceptionally beautiful, cheerful and outgoing child, well
known to the vaqueros of the ranch. Antonio Alvarado has given
us a vivid image of the thirteen-year-old Teresita: "She was tall,
gangly, mostly arms and legs, not nearly as developed as most
Mexican girls her age. Her complexion was fair, her eyes large
and light brown, and her hair thick and long. She was healthy
and exceedingly strong for one her build. I know this because I
fought with her."

Her unusual looks and lively character were bound to attract
attention; even Don Tomás must have noticed the fair-skinned,
laughing child. One account asserts that Teresita, desperate to

escape her aunt's environment, went to Don Tomás, identified herself as his child, and begged for his help. Teresita herself said only that "When I was fifteen, my father sent for me and I went to his hacienda, called Cabora." The year of her arrival at Cabora was 1888.

Don Tomás had sent word to a group of his vaqueros to bring Teresita with them on their way to a roundup near Cabora. The girl made the journey bareback, astride a gentle but spirited horse. Beneath her full skirt, her legs appeared small but well shaped, the ankles slender and the feet narrow and straight. She was barefoot, and the soles of her feet were thick and tough, testimony to years of walking and running without shoes. Teresita's preparations for the occasion were practical and simple. She wore a faded and ill-fitting shirtwaist of the same material as her skirt. Her dark hair, deftly plaited in two long braids, hung over her shoulders in front, falling below her feet as she rode. Around her shoulders and knotted in front was a cotton reboza, once red but now faded to pink with years of washing and exposure to bright sunlight.

The vaqueros watched over her solicitously during the trip, suspecting the import of her trip to Cabora. Teresita had grown up among these gruff and good-natured men. They had taught her to ride and sing *corridos*, or ballads, even teaching her to play the guitar. The results of their expert lessons were evident in Teresita's horsemanship, for she rode with a rhythmic grace and elegant carriage. The trip was a sad one for the vaqueros, who were loath to give up the companionship of this sprightly girl.

Teresita had not been to Cabora since the trip from Sinaloa. As the trail wound through mesquite, paloverde, guayacan, sahuaro and many varieties of yucca, interspersed with patches of grasses, she no doubt was reminded of the Santana ranch in Sinaloa. Eight years had passed since she had left there with her father's caravan, but her recollections must have remained vivid.

The party reached the corral south of the Casa Grande and paused. While Marcos Alvarado gave instructions to the vaqueros,

Teresita looked across the gentle slope leading to the great house and beyond. Marcos alone rode with her to the Casa Grande, naming the various mountain peaks that could not be seen from Aquihuiquichi. Beyond shimmered the blue outlines of several ranges Marcos could not identify. "Too far," he admitted. To the northeast, nearer at hand, he pointed out the jagged, granite-colored escarpments of the Sierra Baroyeca, where there were mines, and the arid hills of Cerro de San Miguel and Sierra de las Vacas. The towering peaks of the Sierra Madre were almost completely lost in the distant haze.

As they passed under the arch at the entrance, Teresita exclaimed at the size and beauty of her father's house. Bougain-villea blossoms formed a band of vivid crimson draped from the lintels of the long veranda on the north side of the compound. The white columns of the arcade along the west wing were surrounded by large clay pots of red and white geraniums. Under hanging baskets filled with masses of ferns stood a wooden cage of brilliantly plumed birds singing gaily—thrushes, parakeets, macaws, canaries and a rare parrot.

Two women, one very old and one very young, sat in the shade of the north veranda. While the old woman sewed with deft fingers, the younger one pushed a cradle suspended from the rafters by four leather thongs. Both looked up expectantly as Teresita and Marcos rode through the wide gate. Presently the old woman reached beside her chair for a homemade crutch and hobbled forward to meet the newcomers. She bade Marcos good day, but her sharp black eyes were reserved for Teresita.

"You are Teresita," she said. "Don Tomás told us you were coming. Get down and let me look at you." Her voice was clear and firm, belying the toothless face etched with wrinkles.

Teresita slid lithely to the ground and stood before the old woman, who surveyed her appraisingly from head to foot. The old one's eyes beheld a figure taller than the average woman on the ranch, with a large, well-shaped head poised above a slim body. The girl's breasts, she noted, were small and just beginning to develop beneath the rude shirtwaist. Something about her slender wrists and hands suggested strength. Teresita's brown eyes, unusually large and set wide apart beneath heavy brows, looked back at the old woman steadily, revealing her anxiety for approval.

After several minutes, she addressed Teresita. "I am Huila. I remember you as a long-legged tomboy who helped to drive the goats from Sinaloa. You have turned out better than I thought possible. Come along."

She hobbled back to the veranda and to Gabriela, who had resumed rocking her swing-cradle. The young mother turned to face Teresita.

"Gabriela," Huila called impishly, "here is your new daughter."

The incongruity of that relationship made both girls smile impulsively. Although they were almost the same age, even a casual observer would have detected considerable differences between the two. Teresita was the taller, and with her long braids, bare feet and peasant dress, she appeared just what she was, an adolescent girl who had just stepped out of a ramada. However, the radiance of her smile and remarkable luster of her eyes more than compensated for her travel-stained clothes and dusty feet. Gabriela, by this time, was a poised and well-rounded young matron. She wore her hair piled high, securing it with an elaborate tortoise-shell comb, and was dressed in handsome style, as befitted the consort of a prosperous *hacendado*.

The two stood taking each other's measure, vaguely sensing the effect each might have on the other's life. Intuitively, they knew they would necessarily become either allies or competitors for the favors of Don Tomás.

"You are welcome to Cabora," Gabriela said softly. Stepping forward, she embraced Teresita with a warmth that implied more than the usual casual greeting. It was the beginning of a close and treasured friendship that was to last for the rest of Teresita's life.

Marcos observed the meeting from his horse. Like the other vaqueros, he was anxious for Teresita's future happiness and well aware that much was at stake in the first encounter of these two people. He was pleased now with what he witnessed. After dismounting, he untied from the back of his saddle the little bundle containing all of Teresita's earthly possessions. She thanked him with a smile warm with gratitude.

As Marcos prepared to leave, he overheard Huila characteristically taking full charge of the situation.

"Don Tomás has gone to Huatabampo and will be away for a week," she told the girl. "In the meantime we will make you presentable." She steadied herself on her crutch and surveyed Teresita with a calculating eye. Then she reached out and took the miserable bundle from the girl.

"Take what you wish. The rest we will give to the women of the vaqueros," she said, as she pitched the bundle against the wall. "We have some cloth here. In a few days we will have you looking like the daughter of the *patrón*."

A mestiza distantly related to the Urreas by marriage, Huila had been a valued member of the household ever since she had been widowed, long before the birth of Don Tomás. She was a woman of much wisdom, and possessed a vast knowledge of herb medicines as well as much experience as a midwife. She could read and write, was skillful with her hands, cooked, and taught many of the Urrea women the art of fine sewing and embroidery. With infinite patience and an air of unyielding authority, she also supervised the *patrón's* sizable coterie of domestics.

Don Tomás regarded her with great respect and saw to it that she joined the exodus from Sinaloa. He installed her as head housekeeper, first at Aquihuiquichi and then at Cabora. But she was much more than an overseer. In addition to supervising the kitchen, the housekeeping, the flowers and birds, the washing and ironing, she administered medicine to the sick and counsel to the lovelorn, and served as arbiter in any disputes that arose in her domain. She did not eat at the table with the family, but dined alone in great dignity at a small table on the veranda, by the kitchen door. The servants ate in the kitchen.

One afternoon a few days after Teresita's arrival, Don Tomás rode into the compound followed by his *peón de estribo*. He handed the reins of his horse to a *mozo*, removed his felt hat and struck it against his leather chaps, raising a small cloud of dust. Then he glanced toward the veranda. Three women stood there, waiting for him. He recognized Huila and Gabriela, but for a moment he was at a loss to identify the tall one. As he walked toward the house he studied her. Slowly her identity registered. Turning to Huila, he inquired, "How did you bring about this transformation?" Without waiting for a reply, he walked quickly to Teresita and gave her a warm embrace and a kiss on the cheek. Then he held her at arm's length and looked her up and down. "My child, you are a joy to behold. I am delighted that you are here!"

Huila's clever fingers had wrought a stunning change. A snugly buttoned, indigo-blue basque, made of cotton cloth with white ruffles at the throat and wrists, emphasized the girl's ripening maturity. Teresita's height was enhanced by a full-draped skirt and a pair of Gabriela's shoes. Her thick hair was wound into a graceful chignon, secured with a comb, giving her an air of elegant poise.

She blushed with pleasure at Don Tomás's obvious approval. He in turn found himself transfixed by her eyes—for the first time becoming aware of their luminous, magnetic quality.

Huila, silent and intent, stood apart and shrewdly gauged the *patrón's* reaction. For thirty years she had watched Tomás respond to attractive women, and seldom had his face revealed such open pride and pleasure. Huila's wise old eyes fastened on Gabriela, straining to detect any hint of jealousy or resentment. But Gabriela's attitude mirrored that of Don Tomás; she was rejoicing, almost on the verge of tears, so proud she was of her own hand in the metamorphosis from peasant girl to graceful young woman. Huila smiled to herself, nodding, as if to say, "This is a good omen."

At the evening meal Don Tomás sat at the head of the long table on the veranda, with Gabriela on his right and Teresita on his left. It was one of the rare occasions when there were no guests for supper. *El patrón* was in high good humor, and the poetic side of his nature, a facet few people suspected because he kept it well hidden, took over completely. His eyes kept traveling from his young mistress to his new-found daughter, both charming and beautiful, yet vastly different. Gabriela, ripe and radiant with the glow of young motherhood, was a symbol of the earth and its bounty, the substance in which the eternal cycle of life ebbs and flows, a fascinating organism reacting to the stimuli of nature, ready to produce and mature. In Teresita, on the other hand, he sensed some rarer substance, something ethereal—an embodied spirit, both vivacious and sensitive. One was of the flesh, the other of the spirit. But these thoughts he kept to himself.

"This occasion requires a celebration," he announced jovially. To Huila he called, "Bring the *mezcal!*"

She sent a maid bearing a jug and three slender crystal glasses. Don Tomás fingered the three glasses and then set two of them aside. "Both of you are still children. I will do the drinking."

With that he downed a generous draft of the potent native liquor, quickly licking the salt sprinkled on the back of his hand and sucking a slice of lime, as was the custom. He became more effusive as the mezcal warmed his spirits. He recited poetry, something Huila had never heard him do before. Tomás then began a song, a ballad of unrequited love, and Teresita joined in, her melodious contralto harmonizing with his deep baritone. He nodded genial approval and encouraged her to carry on to the end of the twenty-two verses.

"Bravo, Teresita! Do you know other songs?"

"A few."

"If we only had a guitar player."

"I play the guitar . . . a little."

"You do? Wonderful! Huila," he called, "send to Alberto's ramada for his guitar!"

The instrument was brought, and Teresita tested the strings until they were tuned to her voice. She tried a turn or two, strumming a few chords. Then her long, slender fingers began to pick the melody of an ancient *corrido* of Sonora. She sang, and Don Tomás joined in with feeling. Their voices carried across the slope and the arroyo to the ramadas of the vaqueros and workers. *Corrido* followed *corrido*, father and daughter taking increasing pleasure in each folk song or love lament shared together.

After a time Huila spoke. "Señor, others are enjoying your songs." She motioned toward the crowd of workers, a hundred or more, respectfully listening outside the house.

The effects of the *mezcal* began to wear off, and Don Tomás, always a temperate man, pushed his glass aside. "Now that we have a singer in the family, life at Cabora is not going to be dull," he said gaily. Then he added, "My child, the next time I go to Guaymas I will buy you the best guitar I can find."

Father and daughter smiled at each other. Although Teresita never asked for anything, and remonstrated gently when he brought her gifts, the new guitar was but the first of many expressions of Don Tomás's love.

Chapter Four

ANTONIO ALVARADO, who saw Teresita almost daily in Sinaloa and as long as she remained at Aquihuiquichi, seldom glimpsed her after she became a member of the family of the *patrón*. Marcos Alvarado came upon her only occasionally, when at the ranch on business. But her half-sister Apolonaria, who visited Cabora from time to time, cherished several memories of Teresita's gradual transformation from an unwanted child in a primitive ramada to the cultivated daughter of the Casa Grande, in its own time the epitome of country elegance.

There was the matter of Teresita's learning to wear shoes. Never having worn a pair of shoes before coming to Cabora, she was as naturally graceful as a deer. She appeared to glide rather than walk, a habit acquired over the years from the humble necessity of carrying pails of water on her head. When Huila insisted that as the daughter of a *hacendado* she must wear elegant, high-heeled pumps, Teresita became as awkward as a newborn calf. Feeling off balance, she tended to walk stiff-legged. Gradually, after much practice and discomfort, the calf again became a gazelle.

Then there was the problem of horseback-riding. Before coming to Cabora she rode with the vaqueros as occasion offered, astride, bareback, barefooted and bare-legged. This she loved. At Cabora she was obliged to ride in a voluminous riding skirt, with lady's boots, on a side saddle, with an escort—never with the vaqueros. Don Tomás gave her a horse she called Gavilán, a beautiful, spirited but gentle animal with flowing chestnut mane and tail. She loved the horse, but fiercely disliked the side-saddle and other trappings.

While, for the most part, Teresita loved the new life, occasionally her longing for the old freedoms, when she could ride with the vaqueros without regard for convention, was overpowering. One day when such a mood was upon her, she ordered her horse saddled. Properly attired, she managed to slip away alone. Teresita rode like a genteel young lady to an open glade on a remote part of the ranch, where she found a spot sheltered on every side by tall *guayacan* bushes. There she dismounted, removed the saddle and blanket, took off her riding boots and stockings, and let her hair down. Then she swung herself onto the horse in one effortless motion and dashed off, astride the astonished Gavilán's back.

Out riding alone that morning, Don Tomás sighted the girl and jerked his horse up short. Across the glade below him galloped Teresita, streaking hell for leather, a vision of grace and rhythm. The horse's nose was extended, nostrils flaring, its mane and tail streaming in the wind. With her head thrown back, catching the wind in her mouth, the girl appeared to be as one with the horse. She rode with her skirt pulled up almost to her thighs, the slender bare legs gripping the horse's sides. The sun caught the red glints of her long, unbound hair as it tossed in the wind behind her. Don Tomás watched with amazement and fascination.

As quickly as it had appeared, the breathtaking apparition sped from his sight. Don Tomás rapidly descended the hill and galloped after her, while attempting to decide what he should say to the girl. By custom young ladies were never permitted to ride alone or in such disarray at any time. His first impulse was

38

to be stern, to reprimand her and command her never to repeat her misdemeanor. Then, recalling similar outbursts from his own youth, he understood the sudden vision of joy and freedom he had just witnessed and weakened in his resolution to play the disapproving father.

As he neared the thicket where she had left her saddle, his mount neighed and was answered by Teresita's horse. Don Tomás called out softly, not wanting to startle the girl. He rode into the hideaway and found Teresita standing barefoot with one arm around the horse's neck, gently stroking Gavilán's nose. The animal's sides were still heaving from the spirited jaunt.

Don Tomás tried to look very severe, shaking his head reproachfully. Had Teresita shown any trace of fear he probably would have chastised her heartily, as was his habit with women. Only his mother had refused to be intimidated by Don Tomás. Now as he regarded his daughter, her luminous, arresting eyes returned his stare without a quiver, and after what seemed an interminable interval, it was he who shifted his eyes. Suddenly he felt completely disarmed. Something in the girl's manner reminded him of his mother, but there was a difference. In any confrontation, Doña Apolonaria reacted with anger, and coercion was futile. Teresita's calm forbearance was even more disarming. Admiration turned his scowl into an indulgent smile.

"It's all right, my child. I myself did even wilder things when I was your age. In the future when you feel the urge to ride with the wind, tell me. I will go with you and keep guard. We won't mention this to anyone."

He dismounted and saddled her horse while Teresita put on her stockings and boots and arranged her clothes and hair. The escapade remained their secret, one more of the multiplying personal ties between father and daughter.

Shortly after Teresita's arrival at Cabora, she was joined by her half-sister Apolonaria Urrea, her three half-brothers, and their illegitimate half-brother, Buenaventura. Don Tomás was trying to make cattlemen of the boys, and during the week they were in the saddle most of the time. But on weekends they stayed at headquarters, full of energy and mischief. Confined to the veranda one rainy weekend, they invited the girls to join them in a game of charades.

It happened that of all the children in Doña Loreto's household, it was Buenaventura who most disliked Teresita. He never lost an opportunity to tease, irritate or try to discredit her. Perhaps as the only other "natural" child in the family, he felt his position threatened by Teresita's acceptance.

Teresita had one scarcely discernible nervous habit. When she was extremely weary or very intent, her left eyelid drooped slightly. When it became Buenaventura's turn to perform a charade, he did an exaggerated and ludicrous impersonation of Teresita—her talk, walk, mannerisms, and even the drooping eyelid. Everyone, including Teresita, thought the act was very funny and laughed openly. Spurred on by his audience's response, Buenaventura carried his exaggerations to the point of ridicule. Teresita's good-natured tolerance vanished. Suddenly she sprang to her feet and confronted him, staring at him without a word. Some powerful, hypnotic force seemed to flow from her large eyes into his, freezing the contortions on his face. At that instant Buenaventura's mouth was cruelly distorted, his left eyelid drooped, and one arm was raised above his head. For a moment everyone thought this paralyzed tableau was all part of the act. Teresita was the first to discover that something inexplicable had occurred. Her anger changed to concern, and the others, realizing that something was amiss, suddenly became very quiet. Buenaventura stood helplessly before them, his arms rigid, his face frozen in a hideous grimace. As puzzled as the others, Teresita put her hand on Buenaventura's cheek and said contritely, "I'm sorry, Buenaventura. Forgive me."

Slowly he relaxed and regained his composure, but the braggadocio had vanished. Crestfallen, he went to one side and sat down. He never tried to badger Teresita again.

Although this event was unusual and a little mysterious,

those present, including Teresita, attached no particular importance to it at the time. All of them had seen thrown horseback riders hit the ground, momentarily stunned, the breath knocked out of them. In a short time they would get up and walk away, shaking off the temporary stupor. What had happened to Buenaventura was assumed by all to be in the same category.

It was during the summer of Apolonaria's visit to Cabora that she and Teresita became friends. Both were about sixteen, an age when the two girls shared many secrets and made giggling plans for their future, full of romantic speculation about the identities of husbands-to-be. Apolonaria noticed nothing out of the ordinary in her companion until Teresita made a most startling prediction.

One day the two of them joined their father for a ride about the ranch. When they came to a fork in the road they met another rider coming from the opposite direction. Neither girl had ever seen or heard of him before, but Don Tomás knew the man and called him by name, introducing him as Señor Gutiérrez. He doffed his expensive-looking hat with a flourish and gave each girl an appraising look and a friendly nod. Then, turning to Don Tomás, he explained that he was interested in buying some cattle and was on his way to Cabora for just that purpose. Don Tomás invited the man to accompany him to headquarters and spend the night. The two rode ahead, leaving the girls to follow. When the men were out of hearing distance, Teresita leaned over and said, "Apolonaria, that is the man you are going to marry."

Apolonaria was speechless with surprise. When she recovered, she asked, "When?"

"In two years and three months," Teresita replied.

Her young friend was impressed by Teresita's matter-of-fact conviction; she made her pronouncement simply and surely, as though forecasting the next day's weather. By the time Apolonaria's marriage took place, exactly two years and three months after her first brief meeting with Gutiérrez, Teresita's powers had outgrown mere fortune-telling, and she performed daily feats that made this simple prediction seem trivial. But for Apolonaria, this was the most astounding one of all.

Because no system of public education existed in Sonora, the most affluent families engaged private tutors, while others, like the Urreas, joined with their neighbors to employ a teacher. The legitimate daughters of Don Tomás received what was then considered proper training for young ladies of prestigious Mexican families. The main objective centered around preparation for marriage and skillful management of the household. They studied reading, writing and simple arithmetic, but considerable emphasis was also placed on conduct, etiquette and the treatment of servants. In all, their training was roughly equivalent to a fifth-grade public school education. Since Teresita never lived with the Alamos branch of her family, she did not receive the instruction given her half-sisters. Instead, she was required to study with her half-brothers. As soon as his sons were old enough to help their father with the ranching, Don Tomás kept them at Cabora, and during slack seasons of cattle work, employed a private tutor for two or three months at a time to teach them the rudiments of scholarship. Teresita, exceedingly precocious, soon outdistanced the boys, much to their frustration and resentment.

One of the formative influences on Teresita's intellectual growth was Lauro Aguirre, the engineer responsible for Cabora's irrigation system. A good friend of Don Tomás, Lauro often visited the Casa Grande on overnight trips from Sinaloa. He held Don Tomás in high esteem, praising his profound grasp of weighty issues despite the lack of formal education. Tomás's library at Cabora was comparable to Don Lauro's, for he had an inquiring and wide-ranging curiosity and acquired books for the pleasure they gave on long, quiet evenings. During Lauro's visits to Cabora, the two men would sit on the veranda until late at night, discussing the oppressive political situation in Mexico, the significance of Mexico's history, its religion and economy, and the ultimate destiny of the republic. Of all the people connected with Cabora, only Teresita showed an interest in these discussions. She would sit quietly, listening to their conversations, usually for as long as they lasted. Aguirre's impression of her at that time was as a well-mannered, attentive and beautiful girl.

Before coming to Cabora, Teresita's days had been filled with humdrum routine. Endless tasks kept her busy: carrying water, cutting firewood, grinding corn on a stone metate, patting out tortillas, washing and ironing clothes, and minding the babies who were added regularly, year after year, to the household. At the Casa Grande, she was not permitted to do any of the menial work. She found the idleness hard to endure, particularly since her new status prohibited her from engaging in such favorite pastimes as riding and singing with the vaqueros. The only diversions permitted her were learning embroidery from Huila and playing with Gabriela's children. Teresita cared not at all for the painstaking art of needlework, and although she loved children, she certainly could not make a full-time diversion out of amusing Gabriela's babies.

For one change she was tremendously grateful. She was free from her nagging, fault-finding aunt. Gabriela was warm and friendly; there was a strong attachment between her and Teresita. Huila was kind and protective toward Don Tomás's daughter. Teresita quickly developed a profound admiration and respect for the wrinkled old woman who so cleverly kept the domestic routine of the hacienda running smoothly.

It was from Huila that she learned the skill that was to lead her toward a destiny she could never have imagined. Huila was a *curandera,* an "herb doctor" who cared for the sick and injured in the three ramada villages surrounding the Casa Grande. Occasionally the skillful old woman was even sent for to attend the critically ill on the other ranches. One day Huila invited Teresita to go with her on her rounds. The girl went, and her affinity for the calling was immediate and intense. She began accompanying Huila on each of her sick calls, and soon these trips became the high points of Teresita's life at Cabora. She observed Huila's techniques of diagnosis and treatment. The old woman's classification of illnesses was simple and straightforward: people had fever, headaches, diarrhea, boils, incurable sores (cancer), colds, measles or one of perhaps a dozen other ailments; all ailing women of childbearing age were first suspected of being pregnant. For each indisposition Huila had a remedy concocted from herbs.

Teresita was fascinated by Huila's medicines, which seemed to effect remarkable results in most of the patients. She was eager to find out how they were made and spent hours in Huila's room, learning from her the names and medicinal properties of a hundred or more herbs. The old woman kept her remedies in stretched bull scrotums, hanging from pegs on the wall. She also had a few specimens of undisclosed curative potential: rennet from the fourth stomach of a cow, a rattlesnake skin and a rabbit's foot. The herbs, Teresita discovered, came from weeds, bushes, berries, grasses, barks, roots of trees and cacti, and seeds of various kinds. Carefully memorizing the names of each, she learned how to recognize the different varieties as well as their individual curative powers.

Huila collected many of these plants on the ranch. Others she obtained by making a trip once a year to Navojoa, where she bought them from an old, grizzled Indian, who had lost one eye over thirty years ago in a fight alongside Benito Juárez against the dictator Santa Ana. He knew the names of every one of his two hundred herbs and what each was supposed to cure. Some of the old man's herbs came from other states and even from across the ocean. He would sell to anyone, but he preferred to market wholesale lots to professional *curanderas*. With each herb he gave free information about its virtues and how to take or apply it.

On one of her trips to Navojoa, Huila took Teresita to see the old vendor. The girl was fascinated by the Indian's vast knowledge, discovering in him the same native wisdom that guided Huila's practiced ministrations. Although he was illiter-

ate, he had an intuitive understanding of the medicinal properties of plants, reinforced by tradition. Such folk remedies were
passed on from generation to generation among the tribes and
became a vital part of each culture.

No one on the ranch, except perhaps Don Tomás, appre-
ciated Huila more than Teresita. For her part, Huila became
increasingly aware of her apprentice's abilities and her influence
on the patients. Not long after Teresita started making calls with
her, she noticed that the girl's presence had a singular effect on
the sick. Although she stood respectfully behind the old woman,
her concern and warmth made them immediately aware of her
presence. When Huila had finished her examination and diagnosis, Teresita would kneel beside the ailing person, touch his
forehead or cheek, and offer some soothing words. Huila's sharp
eyes noted the calming effects of these gestures. At first Huila
said nothing of her observations and assessment of the girl's potential, not even to Teresita. Eventually she told Don Tomás in
strict confidence that Teresita had the makings of a great *curandera*, one who would succeed her at Cabora.

In time, Huila came to depend more and more on Teresita.
One day a child came running to summon the *curandera* to the
ramada of a vaquero. Huila hurried as fast as her crippled leg
permitted, to find a young wife in the throes of a difficult childbirth, her first. Most of the vaqueros' women were part Indian
and endured childbirth with the grim stoicism of that race. But
this patient was scarcely more than a child, only fourteen years
old and not yet fully developed. She was in great pain and cried
out pitifully, biting her fists and writhing violently on top of the
cowhide mat that served as a bed. Huila immediately realized
that she might lose both mother and baby. Her first thought was
to get Teresita's help, and she sent a girl to fetch her. By the time
Teresita arrived the child-mother was nearly comatose: her color
was ashen, she was trembling spasmodically, and her spasms had
become feeble. Teresita knelt down beside her and began stroking her perspiring forehead and cheeks, all the while talking to

her softly. The girl opened her eyes and found herself looking into the serene, dark eyes of Teresita, who, with her steady gaze, seemed to hold the patient entranced. Gradually the young mother relaxed, apparently relieved of the excruciating pain. In a few moments the baby was delivered alive.

A short time later, Teresita again demonstrated her tranquilizing gifts. A vaquero, convulsed with pain, was brought in from the range on an improvised stretcher made of two poles and a poncho. His horse had fallen, and he had suffered a compound fracture of the thigh. Huila directed the men to place him on the long dining table on the veranda and had them remove the injured man's trousers. As she began probing with sensitive fingers to determine the nature of the fracture, the vaquero was wracked with spasms of agonizing pain. Teresita stood by, watching. Remembering her apprentice's strange success during the childbirth episode, Huila asked the girl to calm the writhing man. Teresita looked steadily into the vaquero's eyes, again producing a soothing effect on the suffering patient. Huila probed again, and this time the man did not even flinch. She joined the broken bones and covered the wound with a poultice of leaves that would prevent infection and reduce the swelling. She then fitted the leg with handmade splints kept on hand for just such emergencies. All this time Teresita kept the vaquero under control with her voice and her gaze, never taking her eyes from those of the patient. Yet she seemed to be aware of all that Huila was doing. When Huila had finished, the men carried the vaquero to his ramada. The old woman returned to her chair by the kitchen door and for a long time sat there, lost in thought, slowly shaking her head from side to side. At length she said, scarcely above a whisper, "Teresita, you have something that I do not have."

Others besides Huila were beginning to suspect that Teresita possessed unusual powers. One of these was Josefina Félix, Teresita's most intimate friend during her years at Cabora. The two became acquainted through the Esquerres family, who lived

in Baroyeca and were on close terms with both the Félix and Urrea families. The Esquerreses and Urreas occasionally visited each other, each family enjoying the other's hospitality for two or three weeks at a time. The Urreas met the Félixes during a sojourn at Baroyeca by Don Tomás and his Cabora clan, his first visit there since Teresita had come to live at the Casa Grande.

Josefina was half a head shorter than Teresita, heavier and more sturdily built. They were both healthy and robust, equally strong and active. As their friendship ripened, the two girls enjoyed long visits with each other, either at Baroyeca or at Cabora. Their relationship lasted as long as Teresita lived, and Josefina journeyed to see Teresita even after her friend was expelled from Mexico.

One morning after Teresita had spent the night with Josefina, they awakened in a playful mood and Josefina tried to force her companion out of bed. Ordinarily, she could have picked Teresita up in her arms and lifted her bodily, but this time Teresita stiffened, looked steadily at Josefina, and challenged her.

"Just try to lift me."

Josefina put her arms beneath her friend's body and struggled, but the girl seemed as heavy as a boulder of equal size. Actually Teresita weighed under 110 pounds, but now her body had become dead weight. Josefina then attempted to lift Teresita's head and shoulders, again to no avail. She tried the feet, but could not budge them either. Baffled, she backed away.

"What has happened? I have lifted you many times."

Teresita looked at her mischievously. "Try again."

She did, and this time lifted her smiling companion at once without effort. Josefina was utterly mystified.

"Try again," said Teresita.

Again Josefina found the girl immovable. "How do you do it?" she asked incredulously.

Teresita teased her a few minutes before answering. Finally, she shrugged her shoulders, turned up the palms of her hands, and said, "I do not know how I do it. When I want you to lift me, you can. When I don't want you to lift me, you can't."

This was as much of an explanation as Teresita could offer. They repeated the game many times thereafter, always with the same results. Josefina got others to try lifting Teresita, but even the strongest of them could not move the girl or any part of her body. Soon it became known in Baroyeca and Cabora that if Teresita did not want to be lifted, then no one, not even the burliest ranch hand, could lift her.

Another game the girls played with each other was called *vencidos,* very much like Indian wrestling. Again, Teresita discovered that she could choose to win or lose. When she did not want to be beaten, no amount of leverage could force her arm to the ground or table-top. After the girls discovered this faculty, or power, they conspired to use it on Teresita's half-brothers. Josefina appointed herself Teresita's manager and arranged *vencidos* contests at Cabora between Teresita and the boys, Buenaventura, Antonio, Tomás *hijo* (junior) and Miguel. All were much stronger and heavier than Teresita, but not one could budge her arm during the match. Then Josefina arranged a lifting game. Teresita alternated her weight, letting each of them lift her the first time and then "making herself heavy" on the second try. The boys were dumfounded. All four tried to lift her at once, but with no success. Buenaventura became extremely exasperated, seeking desperately to find an explanation.

"It's her eyes that do it!" he shouted suddenly.

"How can that be?" asked Antonio.

"I do not know, but it is her eyes!"

Some forty years later, in the course of an interview with José C. Valades, Josefina recalled one of the uncanny qualities about Teresita's eyes:

"I do not believe that anyone could have resisted Teresita's eyes in the dark. They had such an irresistible brilliance that people could not gaze at them. But I could, because that is the way she wanted it to be. If someone should see her eyes open in the dark, it would be very bad for them. For that reason, whenever she made an appearance at night, she did so with her eyes closed. With her eyes open she illuminated the entire room."

Chapter Five

TERESITA brought great vitality to the ranch at Cabora. But in 1889, the second year following her arrival at Cabora, the girl suffered so severe a psychological shock that she lapsed into a comatose state for more than three months. The only account of the cause of her seizure comes from José C. Valades, in *La Opinión*. It seems that a young mining engineer by the name of Millán, at Baroyeca, became insanely infatuated with Teresita. She rejected his advances, he went beserk, and then attempted to rape her at Cabora. Teresita reacted violently to this crude assault, lapsing into a seizure that brought her to the edge of death.

Whatever the cause, the seizure was sudden and devastating. Teresita's breathing became slow and scarcely audible, and her pulse was so weak that only the most sensitive fingers could detect any tremor at all in her slender wrists. The girl's jaws were set like a vise. Even Huila, who hovered over her day and night, could not pry them open with her experienced hands. She refrained from forcing any of her concoctions down Teresita's throat lest she strangle.

When the gravity of Teresita's condition became known, a pall settled over the ranch. The people of Cabora were accustomed to sickness and death. Both were accepted as a matter of course, and life continued in spite of such misfortunes. But with Teresita it was different. The *curandera's* lovely apprentice had brought comfort and gaiety to the ramadas of the working people as well as to the Casa Grande.

Don Tomás came and went as though in a trance, seldom leaving the house, and then only for short periods. Two or three times each night he would go to Teresita's room and stand looking down at his daughter, lying so still on her high, carved bed. Pale and stiff, her features assumed the classic beauty of cold marble. The women kept her luxuriant hair neatly brushed and stretched so that it reached to her feet and outlined her slender form. Don Tomás would always feel her pulse, but lacking a sensitive touch, he could detect nothing. He watched closely to see if she were breathing, never trusting his eyes or ears. Finally leaving the room, he would shake his head at the mystery of her illness and curse his own helplessness. As the days passed, her color became more ashen. Never once did she move a muscle or try to swallow.

Work on the ranch practically ceased. Women from the ramadas came and hovered about the door of Teresita's room, vaguely hoping that their presence and concern would somehow be transmitted; or else they stood in groups along the veranda talking in hushed tones. There was nothing they could do; they could not even give the girl a sip of water. Their only recourse was to pray. Sometimes as many as a dozen women knelt at her bedside, rebozos pulled low over their foreheads, faces drawn and sad, fingering their rosaries and silently moving their lips. Vaqueros from the other ranches rode up to the Casa Grande, inquired after Teresita's condition, lingered a while, and then quietly rode away. Reluctant to disturb the hushed atmosphere of the house, they never went near her room.

A doctor of sorts who lived near Baroyeca was sent for by Don Tomás. After giving the girl a cursory examination, he made his report. Her heartbeat was so feeble that he could barely hear it through his stethoscope. Her breathing was equally faint; even a mirror held to her nostrils revealed almost no trace of respiration. There was nothing, the doctor told Don Tomás, to be done—the girl was living on her "reserve vitality." With no intake of fluids, her body was becoming severely dehydrated, and it was only a matter of time before the life slipped out of her completely. Offering his condolences to Don Tomás, he departed.

Each day, Teresita's skin became more shriveled and her lips more parched and dry. Don Tomás directed the women to keep wet cloths over her mouth. Drawing on her knowledge of external remedies, Huila applied cool poultices to the girl's forehead, neck and shoulders.

On the twelfth day after the seizure, Don Tomás, now utterly devoid of hope, directed the ranch carpenters to construct a coffin. By this time, all routine on the ranch had ceased, the fields were unattended, the cattle milled in the gathering pens, the horses lazed in the corrals. The compound of the Casa Grande was crowded with workers and their women, waiting in small groups and talking in hushed tones.

The next evening Don Tomás again sat beside his daughter and held her wrist, vainly searching for a pulse. While holding the girl's limp hand, he discovered that her formerly rigid fingers were now flexible. He tested her arm and found he could bend it. Eagerly he again felt for her pulse, but the skin remained cold and lifeless to the touch. Desperate for some sign of breath or warmth, he placed his ear against her chest. Teresita's heart was still. Turning to Huila, he softly told her the girl was dead and asked her to have the women prepare the body for burial. As Don Tomás started to leave the room, he remembered the custom of holding a wake. Pausing at the threshold, he directed Huila to have the corpse placed on a table in the room until morning, when it would be placed in the coffin.

Huila took full charge of the situation. The body, completely flexible now, was washed and clothed in a white dress. There was no problem fitting the garment. The hands were folded across the chest and tied with a pale blue ribbon. A little color had come into the cheeks, and the expression of the features was peaceful and serene.

Teresita's mortal remains were placed on the table with lighted candles at the head and foot. When all was ready, Huila gave the arrangements a final inspection and with resignation said, "She is with the angels now."

That evening the wake for Teresita began. As many women as could get into the room knelt and prayed, fondling their beads. Outside the house, fires were built on the far side of the compound, and in the flickering light, shadowy figures of men could be seen standing in small groups, with hats pulled down over their foreheads as they talked in low voices. At midnight, coffee and food were served by the women, who had been taking turns kneeling in Teresita's room.

Later in the night, at what was called "the witching hour," a vaquero's wife raised her bowed head when a candle at the head of the table flared up suddenly, brightly illuminating Teresita's face. The woman saw a movement in the girl's eyelids and froze with fright. Speechless, she could not take her gaze from the face. Then to the woman's shocked amazement, both of Teresita's eyes seemed to open. The woman was transfixed. She could not bring a sound from her throat. She remembered then that a dead person's eyes open unless weights are placed on them. But just as she fastened on this explanation, she saw Teresita's body slowly rise to a sitting position. Finding her voice, the woman screamed. The other mourners, intent on their prayers, were totally unaware of what had taken place until the woman's scream penetrated the silence. Looking up, they beheld Teresita sitting on the table, her open eyes slowly moving from one face to another. Terrified by this ghastly sight, the women made a frantic rush for the door. All but Huila. She did not move.

Teresita looked steadily at the old *curandera,* and then, glancing down, noticed that her wrists were crossed and tied with a ribbon. "What does this mean?" she asked in a barely audible whisper.

Until now, the old woman had been unable to speak. Great drops of perspiration covered her forehead.

"My child," she replied hoarsely, "you were dead."

"Dead?"

"Yes, I prayed as I never did before to the Blessed Virgin to give you back to us. She heard me. You are alive again!"

"The Blessed Virgin? She was here. I talked with her. She told me many things that I must do." Teresita noticed the empty coffin at the end of the room. "Tell Papa I will not need that, but to save it. In three days there will be a use for it."

A rustling noise near the doorway attracted Huila's attention. Some of the frightened women had crept back; a few stood wide-eyed inside the door. As far behind them as Huila could see there were women and men straining to make certain of what they saw and heard. She recognized the *peón de estribo*.

"Cosimero, go quickly and bring Don Tomás!"

Chapter Six

WHEN NEWS of Teresita's astounding return from the dead was brought to him, Don Tomás was overwhelmed with joy. Forgetting to put on his boots, he rushed to the girl's room and stood there, barefoot and speechless, dumfounded at the sight of his daughter sitting up and talking. His first thought was that she must be hungry after fourteen days without food. He called to the cook, who was crowding into the entranceway with the other servants, to hurry and prepare some broth.

"And make it with bull's meat!" Don Tomás shouted after her, as the cook pushed her way through the crowd toward the kitchen. Local tradition decreed that the flesh of a bull was far more potent than that of a cow or steer.

Eventually the broth was prepared and brought, but Teresita paid no attention to the steaming bowl set before her. When Huila urged her to drink, she seemed not to hear. The old woman then fed it to her with a spoon. She swallowed without effort, but made no move to feed herself. After Teresita had consumed the entire bowl, she slept, peacefully and naturally, her pulse and breathing normal. The next day as well she showed no interest in food or dirnk, but swallowed without protest when fed. She was stronger now and sat on the side of the bed. After a while she was able, with the help of Don Tomás, to stand on her feet for a few minutes, but still she made no effort to feed herself.

On the third morning after Teresita's recovery, Huila was found dead in her room. She had passed away quietly in her sleep, with no sign of struggle or discomfort. The indomitable old woman of the Casa Grande was buried in Teresita's coffin, with all the workers and their families gathered at the ranch cemetery to hear a simple service conducted by Don Tomás. Considerable speculation ensued as to the cause of Huila's death, but the consensus was that she was simply worn out, and that the tension during the fourteen days of Teresita's seizure was too much for her frail old body. The tremendous shock of Teresita's revival had mercifully finished her off.

When Teresita was told of Huila's death, she showed no surprise or emotion. Those who knew of the close relationship between the old *curandera* and her apprentice were at a complete loss to explain this absence of grief. The girl's bland indifference, coupled with her earlier prediction of an impending need for the coffin, foreshadowed a series of strange events to come.

As the days passed, Teresita grew more and more abstracted. She would have gone indefinitely without food or drink had Gabriela not taken complete charge of feeding her and tending to her other personal needs. Physically, she reacted to nourishment and care. She could walk without tiring or shortness of breath. She recognized people, but her former mirth and high spirits had disappeared. She never laughed. The mischievous twinkle in her eyes had vanished. Gossip or news of current happenings on the ranch aroused neither interest nor comment. In all, her outgoing and sympathetic disposition seemed to have disappeared or turned inward. Even her expressive eyes appeared fixed on some inner landscape, visible only to Teresita.

Her condition was the main topic of discussion among the people of the ramadas. They were deeply concerned, but could not comprehend this total absence of spirit. Many concluded that the girl had become crazed. As if tragedy had struck one of their own children, the residents of Cabora reacted with worried dismay, never once alluding to her behavior in flippant or denigrating terms.

Don Tomás, although perplexed and anxious, ascribed her condition to the shock of the seizure. He hopefully assured everyone that time and nature would mend the damage. Each day he tried to interest Teresita in the numerous details of ranch life that had previously formed the basis of their animated discussions. He told her about the work of the vaqueros, the young corn growing in the irrigated fields, her horse Gavilán, the new babies in the villages, the antics of the young goats, and the news from the other ranches. None of these familiar subjects aroused any response. While Don Tomás talked, his daughter silently regarded him with her grave, deepset eyes. She seemed totally preoccupied, as if trying to remember something from the distant past. Her expression remained enigmatic and unfathomable.

As time went on, she began to talk rather strangely about the visitation, God and love. The visitation seemed to weigh heavily on her. Don Tomás, perhaps the last person on earth to believe in miraculous visitations, sensed that this might be one subject on which he could get a response. Little by little he drew from her the details of this mysterious visitation. It was obvious that throughout the period of physical collapse, her mind had been unusually active. A dream, or vision, or mental apparition, or some other manifestation had left a vivid and clearly remembered impression.

The Virgin Mary, she said, had appeared and talked to her. She told the girl that she possessed some unusual powers, and that she should use them to help people, to cure them, to comfort and console them. This was God's message. The powers would be revealed to her from time to time.

Don Tomás knew from his experience and reading that all manner of fantastic sequences occur in dreams—even nightmarish experiences with no apparent foundation in reality. He gave no credence to Teresita's disclosures. In his own mind, he was convinced that dreams are recalls, or flashbacks, of past experiences and thoughts. The sequences might be confusing, tangled or irrational, but memory cells in the brain could recall only bits and pieces that had been observed, acted or thought. Repeatedly he tried to explain this to his daughter. She was adamantly convinced that she had seen the Holy Virgin. She also had much to say about the voice. "Whose voice?" Don Tomás asked time and again. "Was it the Holy Mother's or was it some disembodied voice?" Teresita could or would not identify the speaker, but she signified that she fully understood the message and its meaning.

Repeatedly Don Tomás questioned her to discover what the voice had told her. Teresita used different approaches in trying to explain, but each explanation returned to the same theme of curing the sick, consoling those who could not be cured, and comforting those who grieved. All this was the will of God.

These exchanges ended where they began. Don Tomás continued to attribute her lack of logical reasoning to the effects of her illness, and he remained patient, convinced that a full recovery was imminent. Her physical condition was improving; surely time would restore her mental powers and values.

Teresita's preoccupied state persisted. Unless someone held a spoon to her lips, she would not eat. Gabriela still helped her dress and kept her hair neatly brushed and braided. Only one change in her behavior seemed significant. Whether because of a subconscious association with Huila and the sick calls or a compulsion to heed the directions of the voice, Teresita inquired about the sick people on the ranch. When Gabriela told her that the wife of a vaquero was suffering from a fever, Teresita immediately announced that she would go and see the woman. Don Tomás, afraid that she might have a seizure or wander off, had given strict instructions that Teresita should never leave the house without an attendant. Gabriela sent a maid to accompany the girl and keep an eye on her.

Even after weeks of confinement to the house, Teresita's sense of direction was still accurate, and she went straight to the vaquero's ramada. A group of solicitous people was there. Ignoring them, the girl stooped down to examine the ailing woman, who lay on a mat of split carrizo, moaning softly as flies swarmed around her head. Those gathered inside the hut stood back at a respectful distance, watching with mixed reactions. Most of the working people were illiterate and superstitious, credulous believers in the supernatural. To them, Teresita's presence was evidence of a miracle. Some had actually seen her "resurrected from the dead" and believed that her recent strange behavior stemmed from some mysterious possession—by what they did not know. They looked on with trepidation when Teresita knelt beside the sick woman.

The woman herself grew fearful as she saw Teresita bending over her. When the girl took her hand, she trembled from head to foot. Her lips went tight and her jaw stiffened as if she felt a mild shock. Teresita's calm voice soon reassured the patient. Gradually she responded to the hypnotic force of Teresita's eyes. Her fears vanished, and she was oblivious to everything except the presence of the girl. Teresita sent the maid back to the Casa Grande for the herb Huila had used to cure fevers. With it she made a potion, which she bade the woman drink. The woman obeyed, and then lay quietly on the mat.

Teresita and her attendant departed, leaving the woman in the care of her astonished neighbors and relatives. The vaquero's wife raised the hand that Teresita had held and looked at it, puzzled. In stumbling language, she tried to explain the sensation she had felt as the girl touched it. A quiver had passed through her body, a sensation she had never before experienced. By the next day her fever was gone. No one could be sure whether the illness had run its course and would have abated anyway, or whether the herb medicine cured it, or whether Teresita had indeed used some unusual power. The workers on the ranch gave Teresita full credit for the woman's recovery.

The incident inspired a great deal of talk and was no doubt exaggerated with each retelling. As Huila's gentle and precocious assistant, Teresita had been well loved by these people. Now Teresita had changed. Her subdued personality, her abstraction, and her newly acquired powers made her seem strange and inexplicable. Some thought she was demented. Others contended that she possessed supernatural powers. Whatever the people thought of her, they did not deny her entrance to their ramadas. She began making sick calls every day, and became Huila's successor.

Among those who believed she possessed strange powers was Simón Salcedo, a vaquero crippled by a kick in the head by a horse. The man's right leg was stiff, his right arm useless, and the right side of his face was drawn and distorted. Dragging his right leg in the dust, he walked laboriously with a stick in his good hand, cringing at the children's jokes and mockery. The "miracle of the resurrection" and the exaggerated reports of her curing the vaquero's wife convinced him that she might help him also.

Simón sought her out in the village, where she was making her rounds, and pleaded with her to make him whole again. Teresita knew of his condition and was aware that the affliction could not be cured with herbs; otherwise Huila would have helped him long ago. She did not know what to say to the man. As the girl listened to his plea, she was deeply moved by Simón's earnestness and faith. In her compassion, she took his crippled hand in hers and turned her luminous eyes upon him. He felt the same magnetic impulse that the sick woman had reported. Teresita talked to him in a low and soothing voice, inducing a sort of hypnotic trance. Then, reaching to the ground, she picked up some dust and spat in it. She mixed the saliva with the dust, making a paste which she rubbed on the man's leg, arm and face. Those standing by later said that her spittle was red, the color of blood. She took the man's stick from him and told him to walk. This he did. Then she directed him to raise his right hand.

J. CISNEROS

Slowly he lifted his once useless arm. She asked him to smile, and the muscles on the right side of his face responded. In a few days, Simón's face appeared completely normal. Gradually the vaquero began to ride, rope with his right arm, and accomplish all the chores he had not performed for years. According to many witnesses, this was Teresita's "first miracle."

News of the event spread rapidly to the other Urrea ranches, where Teresita was well known. With the exception of Don Tomás, the people of the ranches accepted the cure as a miracle. The *patrón* admitted that Simón had been cured, but not by a miracle. It was done, he insisted, by the power of suggestion. Nature, he said, had slowly repaired the damage. Simón had simply become accustomed to living as a cripple; the limp and distorted facial muscles were a matter of habit. He could have regained the use of the afflicted parts himself if he had worked at doing so.

In the oral and written accounts of this period, several other "first miracles" have been reported. In his book, Lauro Aguirre told of another early cure, calling it the "first miracle." A woman, Señora Rosario Bajo, suffered what was thought to be a hemorrhage of the lungs. Bleeding profusely, she was in agonizing pain when brought to Teresita, who put her into what could have been a hypnotic trance. Then she said to the woman, "I will cure you with the blood of my heart," repeating the dust and blood-tinged saliva treatment. Immediately, according to Aguirre, the bleeding ceased; the cure was complete.

Teresita herself later described one of the early cures in an interview with a reporter from the *New York Journal,* in 1901. "Those who saw told me later that an Indian woman was brought to me to be cured. One leg was paralyzed, and she had not walked for a year. I placed my hands on the paralyzed part and told her to walk. Poor woman! She was afraid to try. She cowered and cried, but I insisted. She took one step tremblingly, then another and another. When she found she could walk, she ran back, raised her hands to heaven and cried, 'Santa Teresa!' It was thus that I was named."

Teresita's state of abstraction lasted over three months. During this period she was fed, bathed and dressed. Her hair was combed and arranged for her. Solemn and preoccupied, she seemed to be listening constantly to her inner voice. Only when commanded by some secret prompting to visit the sick and crippled did she find the initiative to get up and leave the house.

Suddenly, overnight, the fog enshrouding her mind cleared. One morning, as Gabriela carried Teresita's breakfast into her room, the girl greeted her with a cheery "Good morning." Gabriela found this unusual, since Teresita had not greeted her so positively since before the seizure. When she pulled up a chair to the bedside and prepared to feed her charge, Teresita reached out, grabbed the platter, and indignantly said, "I can feed myself!" As the girl hungrily devoured the food before her, Gabriela watched, perplexed, realizing there had been a change, but unable to determine the extent of Teresita's recovery. When Teresita had finished and thanked her for bringing the breakfast, she asked, "Why did you do this? I can come to the table like everyone else."

To Gabriela's surprise, the girl began to chat casually about events that had happened over three months ago, as though recalling people and incidents of only yesterday. Then she got out of bed, went to the mirror, unbraided her hair, and brushed and arranged her floor-length tresses with no difficulty, while Gabriela stood protectively near. After she had dressed herself, she said, "Now I must go with Huila to visit the sick."

Gabriela suddenly wondered how completely Teresita had recovered. "Don't you remember?" she asked.

"Remember? Remember what?"

"Huila is dead."

Stunned, Teresita sat down abruptly. "Dead? When did it happen? Why didn't you tell me?"

"You have been very ill, Teresita."

Gabriela related all that had occurred during the girl's memory lapse. It was clear that Teresita did not know either about the seizure or about anything that had happened afterward.

On that day her recovery became complete. It was as if she had suddenly returned from a world of melancholia and withdrawal into one of awareness, self-command and normal buoyant spirits. The sparkle returned to her eyes and the swift, vivacious smile to her lips. But it was some time before she could fully understand all that had transpired during her illness.

She was amazed and perplexed when Gabriela told her of the marvelous cures, scarcely believing her friend's vivid recital. Gabriela seemed to be describing the actions of someone other than herself. To convince her, Simón Salcedo, Señora Rosario Bajo and the woman with the paralyzed leg were brought to the house to tell their stories. On seeing them recovered, and fully realizing the enormity of her cures, she was overcome with humility. The experience left her subdued and mystified.

For days Teresita pondered the significance of what she had seen and heard. Suddenly she wondered whether she still possessed these powers, or if they were some strange quirk of her illness that had departed as soon as she recovered. In the days that followed, members of the household described to Teresita her trance-like discourses on religion, the visitation of the Holy Virgin and the voice. She asked many questions, and they told her as much as they could. She tried hard to recall, but remembered nothing. Soon all the events began to shape themselves into a pattern, then a revelation. These powers to heal and to cure, if she still possessed them, were gifts from God, to be used with humility and without material reward.

Chapter Seven

DON TOMAS would have no part in revealing to Teresita all the strange happenings during her seizure and the period that followed. Nor was he aware of what others had told her and the effects of these revelations upon her. When he realized that Teresita was fully recovered, his joy was as great as when she had "come alive" a few months earlier. The nightmare of that experience and the ensuing period of abstraction were over. Life on the ranch would return to normal. There would be singing, gaiety and laughter. Teresita would again become the sparkling catalyst of the household, and the harmonious routine of the Casa Grande prior to her illness could be resumed. Determined to blot out those troubled three and a half months, Don Tomás avoided any talk of mysterious cures or babble about voices and visitations.

He was aware of what had happened to Simón Salcedo, Señora Bajo and the Indian woman with the paralyzed leg, but he still attributed these cures to the power of suggestion, an explicable natural phenomenon. Now that Teresita was back to normal, she could, if she wished, take up Huila's practice of visiting the sick and dispensing herbs. But he wanted no more so-called miracles or references to saints.

During the next few weeks, Teresita began to take an active

part in family diversions. Although she was often thoughtful and serious, she played the guitar, sang, joked, performed mimicry and enjoyed the merry-making. Of all the family, only her brothers remained a little in awe of her, still remembering what she had done to Buenaventura, as well as her recent strange behavior. Their uneasiness was not entirely without cause, for in spite of Don Tomás's efforts to restore the happy atmosphere, there were small ruptures in the otherwise smooth routine of the Casa Grande that made him apprehensive.

One such incident occurred during the noonday meal at the long table on the veranda. Don Tomás presided at the head of the table, with his daughter to his right. Throughout the meal, Teresita took an active and animated part in the conversation. Then, suddenly, her voice trailed off in mid-sentence. Don Tomás looked at her curiously, and saw that her features seemed frozen and trance-like. For a moment he watched her, fearful that another attack was imminent. Noticing her stiff posture and blank stare, the others also grew quiet and anxious. Gabriela rose from her seat at the foot of the table and came to stand behind Teresita's chair, ready to help the girl in case she collapsed or became rigid. The trance lasted only a few minutes. Immediately upon coming out of it, Teresita turned to her father.

"Papá, Antonio Alvarado is on his way here from Aquihuiquichi. There has been an accident over there. He is coming for help."

This pronouncement, delivered out of the blue, made a profound impression on everyone at the table. Don Tomás, puzzled as were the others, asked, "How do you know?"

"Because I have just seen Antonio coming this way, riding under whip."

This sounded so incredible that Don Tomás feared his daughter had withdrawn to her abnormal condition. His uneasiness was soon allayed; Teresita resumed the conversation where she had left off. Everyone present discounted the prediction as one of her odd quirks and gave it no further thought. Before the family left the table, however, Antonio galloped up the road from Aquihuiquichi, astride a horse covered with lather. Don Tomás hurried out to meet him.

A horse had fallen, Antonio breathlessly told him, and badly mangled a vaquero's leg. The *mayordomo* urgently asked that Teresita come and do what she could for the leg. Teresita listened to the report and, without waiting for her father's reaction, rushed to change to her riding skirt and gather the herbs, splints and bandages she knew Huila would have used. Don Tomás ordered horses saddled for himself and Teresita, as well as a fresh mount for Antonio, and the three took off within minutes. When they arrived, Teresita adjusted the broken bones, applied splints, and administered special herbs to prevent swelling and infection, all just as Huila would have done. The major difference was that Teresita placed the man under hypnosis, preventing the pain that had been endured during Huila's ministrations.

The treatment finished, Don Tomás and Teresita left. On the road to the Casa Grande, the *patrón*'s thoughts returned to his daughter's pronouncement. How could she have known about Antonio's coming before he had gotten there? He tried to elicit from her some rational explanation. Teresita's reply did little to help her father out of his dilemma.

"I just saw him coming at a fast gallop, and I knew he would not be treating a horse like that unless something dreadful had happened."

Don Tomás said no more to his daughter about the mystery, but he was troubled by the incident for days afterward. No plausible explanation suggested itself to him, no matter how long he pondered the event. He could not put it out of his mind.

A month passed. One Sunday afternoon a number of visitors were gathered on the veranda of the Casa Grande. At the request of Don Tomás, Teresita sang some ballads, accompanying herself on the guitar. After she had finished, the friends began complimenting her on her performance. Suddenly she fell into a trance, similar to the one preceding Antonio's urgent arrival a few weeks earlier. The visitors were perplexed but hesitant to say or do anything. Trusting that the outcome would be no more threatening than on the previous occasion, Don Tomás made a motion with his hand, signaling that there was no cause for alarm. But the trance lasted longer than before. When it passed, Teresita's normally mobile and happy features were grave and troubled.

"Papá, there will be a tornado at the ranch of Las Vacas next Thursday afternoon. You must send someone to tell those people not to be there that day."

"Do not trouble yourself," Tomás said gently. "There is no way to predict the future." Unlike the first pronouncement, this foretold some natural disaster in the future, not one that had already happened. Don Tomás rapidly considered the differences between the two predictions and concluded that this second prophecy was utterly preposterous.

"But, Papá, you must do something," Teresita pleaded anxiously.

For a day Don Tomás mulled over his choices. He could not bring himself to accept his daughter's predictions of the future. Nor could he dismiss this prognostication without a second thought, since she had, after all, been accurate in the first instance. By the third day he decided it was safer not to take chances. If no tornado appeared, the residents of Las Vacas would suffer nothing more serious than some minor inconveniences. If it did sweep through the area, however, much harm and tragedy could result unless the people were evacuated. He rode to Las Vacas, ordered the vaqueros to load their scant possessions on wagons, and sent them with their families to Aquihuiquichi.

Don Tomás accompanied the group and spent the night at Aquihuiquichi. The next day he studied the skies carefully, keeping a sharp watch for dangerous cloud patterns. He noted

J. CISNEROS

the usual cumulus thunderheads, normal for that time of year, but none of these appeared especially threatening. Later in the afternoon, however, one of the innocent-looking cloud masses shaped itself into a tornado, and within minutes, its funnel was sweeping across the land in the vicinity of Las Vacas. Immediately Don Tomás and his vaqueros took off in that direction. On arriving they found the vaqueros' ramadas in shambles: some had disappeared completely, with not a post or beam in sight. Whole sections had been utterly obliterated.

Don Tomás had witnessed now a second, even more confounding, demonstration of his daughter's prophetic insights. Yet the girl's prediction and the appearance of the tornado could have been sheer coincidence, he thought. The odds were one in a thousand, maybe one in a million. But such coincidences did happen. Don Tomás could not bring himself to believe that any person could predict the erratic behavior of the elements four days in advance. He returned home and commended Teresita fervently for having saved the families at Las Vacas, but said nothing more about it.

A few days later at breakfast Teresita fell into yet another trance. When it passed, Don Tomás could tell by her expression that the news was good.

"Papá, your friend Don Lauro Aguirre will be here tonight."

This was indeed happy news, if true. Of all his friends, there was no one Don Tomás would rather see and talk with at this juncture than Lauro Aguirre, the wisest, most scholarly, most trustworthy man he knew.

Late that afternoon, Don Lauro arrived on a mule, with a small bundle tied behind the saddle and double leather saddlebags attached to the pommel. One bag held a Bible, a copy of Comte's *Positive Philosophy* and writing materials. The other side contained a six-shooter, surveying instruments and a surveyor's notebook. A deeply religious man of the Methodist faith, Aguirre took little stock in presentiments, adoration of saints, miraculous revelations or the interposition of the priesthood. However, he was a tolerant, as well as a learned, man.

In the evening, after Teresita and the rest of the family had retired, the two friends sat on the veranda and talked late into the night. Don Tomás related the startling events that had occurred on the ranch since Lauro's visit several months earlier. He described Teresita's seizure, the period of self-absorbed preoccupation, and her recent extraordinary predictions. Don Tomás confessed that the latest events baffled him the most. He explained in detail the coming of Antonio, the foretelling of the tornado and the visit of Don Lauro himself. He wondered if Lauro could provide any explanation.

The latter eagerly replied that he had read everything he could find concerning this type of phenomenon. The first and third incidents, it seemed to him, fell into one particular category. Before the invention of the telegraph by Samuel Morse in the 1830s, these experiences had been known as thought transference, clairvoyance or mind reading. After the telegraph came into use, the term mental telepathy became popular, probably because of the analogy to the transmission of messages over wires. Some persons with sensitive nervous mechanisms could send thought waves over considerable distances, provided the sender and receiver were attuned to each other. Such phenomena, Lauro added, had been scientifically verified. As for the tornado, he was unable to offer any rational explanation. The gift of prophesy had been on record since Old Testament times, but modern psychical researchers were not in agreement about the nature and source of such powers, or if, indeed, they actually existed. If there was such a thing, he was sure it was produced by still undiscovered natural laws. He himself believed that prophetic visions did occur, and that Teresita, since she was endowed with unusual sensitivity, could be one of those rare persons attuned to whatever forces made prognostication possible. Some day, he was certain, the natural or supernatural laws governing this phenomenon would be revealed.

Don Lauro had much more to say about the occult, and Don Tomás found himself more inclined to accept this new manifestation of Teresita's formidable abilities. He made no effort to tell his daughter of Don Lauro's explanations. Teresita, for her part, was not concerned about rationalizations and had not given the matter a second thought. To her the most natural thing was to use the powers granted to her; and use them she did.

Chapter Eight

AFTER HIS DISCUSSION with Lauro Aguirre, Don Tomás was more reconciled to Teresita's power of prediction, but his sense of foreboding grew stronger. Intuition told him that life at Cabora would never again be the same. Reports of the amazing occurrences at the ranch were bound to spread. There was no way of knowing how far and wide the news would reach and what reactions these reports would provoke, but Don Tomás could not rid himself of a sense of trouble in the making.

News of the "miracles" did spread, slowly at first, then with increasing speed. By foot, burro, horseback, oxcart, carriage and wagon train, travelers carried stories of La Niña de Cabora south into Sinaloa and Nayarit, east into the high sierras of Chihuahua, and north to the Arizona border. The extent of Teresita's miraculous powers grew with the telling. It was said that she herself had been raised from the dead and, while dead, had talked with the angels and the Holy Mother. She could cure every manner of affliction. She could foretell the future. She could see people and things at great distances, even beyond mountain ranges. She could read one's thoughts from afar. Though fragile and slender, the girl could will herself to become stronger than any man and make herself so heavy that several men could not lift her. With her voice and her eyes she could strike a grown man down as if he were dead. She was recovered from a strange sickness and was now overflowing with compassion for the poor and the afflicted. She was the embodiment of beauty and goodness. Above all, she refused to take payment for her cures. The sick, the lame and the mentally disturbed—and their families—took heart. All became obsessed with one thought: how could they get to Cabora?

Don Tomás's uneasiness following Lauro's visit was justified. The deluge began as a mere trickle, a family or two bringing their ailing ones; the trickle became a small stream with scores arriving each day. The stream grew larger with pilgrims coming by the hundreds, and finally by 1891 the stream swelled to a flood. Pilgrims numbering in the thousands converged on the ranch at one time. A newspaper reporter from Las Cruces, New Mexico, estimated the crowd at five thousand the day he was there in November 1891. A reporter from *El Nacional* in Mexico City put the number at approximately ten thousand at the time of his visit in May 1892. Antonio Alvarado, years later, recalled that on an average day in 1891 the number was about two thousand. However, he added, on Teresita's birthday, October 15, 1891, the crowd was exceedingly large, possibly ten thousand.

As the stream of pilgrims grew steadily larger, Don Tomás's frustration and misgivings increased in proportion to the number of unwanted callers trespassing on his property each day. In vain he pleaded with Teresita not to receive these afflicted people. If only she would make herself unavailable, they and their escorts would eventually go away. Reports of the futility of seeing her would spread and the massive invasions would diminish. But his entreaties were to no avail. Teresita's compassion for the poor, wretched country people with their tattered clothing and sad, imploring eyes was overpowering. Many of them had walked for miles carrying the ailing on litters. When she beheld these trusting and simple believers, her heart went out to them in pity. The instructions of the voice far outweighed the pleas of a stern, demanding and disapproving father. The more he insisted that she give up her treatments, the more adamant she became in making herself accessible to those who sought her help.

At the outset, Teresita received her patients on the spacious veranda. After quickly determining the nature of each illness, she followed the general pattern of treatment learned from Huila, but with special healing powers the old *curandera* had known to be beyond her. From all accounts, Teresita was evidently psychic. Apparently she could not only see and accurately diagnose physical symptoms, but she could also ascertain what was in the minds of the patients and of those closely associated with them. If the ailment was only physical, she used herbs. If the problem was in the person's mind or stemmed from some nervous disorder, Teresita resorted to a token application of saliva mixed with dust. When successful, the cure was effected through hypnotic suggestion, body magnetism and other inexplicable powers.

Teresita could determine almost instantly if an ailment was beyond her competence to cure. In such cases, she offered no false hopes, extending instead what consolation she could to the patient and his family. Most effective, both for those whose ailments were curable and those who were beyond help, was the aura of her presence, both physical and spiritual.

One of the aspects of Teresita's presence that most impressed those who received her ministrations was a perfume emanating from the pores of her skin. Even her perspiration seemed scented with this rare odor. The characteristic did not become particularly noticeable until after her seizure. But whenever, following the illness, she was tense or concentrating intently on a patient, a fragrance filled the area around her, as if someone had opened a bottle of fine cologne. The effect was instantaneously soothing.

A considerable number of Teresita's cures were spectacular, especially those dealing with various forms of paralysis and other disorders of the nervous system. Patients arriving on stretchers or in bull carts, who had not been ambulatory for years before the treatments, arose and walked without assistance. Each cure of this kind was heralded as a miracle by those who witnessed it. Time after time, the patient and family fell on their knees before Teresita and kissed her hand, repeating over and over, "Santa Teresa." Time and again she raised the grateful worshippers to their feet, firmly rejecting the title of saint and repeating that she was just an ordinary person using the powers God had given her. Only to God, she said, should they kneel. Each day the number of pilgrims grew larger, spilling from the veranda and patio to the grounds beyond the Casa Grande.

One afternoon an oxcart arrived at Cabora. A man in his forties walked beside the oxen, periodically casting anxious looks at his wife, who rested in the cart on a thick bed of straw. She was in her middle twenties, a comely young woman with an arresting but pallid face. Some two years earlier the woman had contracted a fever that left her paralyzed from the waist down. With each lurch of the cart, her mouth twisted in pain.

When the two came within sight of the Casa Grande, the man stopped the oxen and surveyed the scene before him. From the crowd of people in the compound, he concluded that this was where La Santa was performing her blessed work. His wife raised herself painfully on one elbow and peered through the heavy stays of the oxcart. The man went to the rear of the cart, lifted her in his strong arms and carried her through the gate into the compound. At the edge of the crowd of two hundred or more, he paused awkwardly, finding no way to get through the crowd with his crippled wife. Then he heard someone call his name. "Fortunato Avendano, bring your wife to me on the veranda." The voice was clear and resonant.

Fortunato was mystified. He had never seen La Santa, and he was sure she had not seen him come into the compound. How

could she have known that he and his wife, Mariana, were at Cabora? He heard the voice again, this time addressing the people.

"Please, my friends, open up a passage so that Fortunato Avendano may bring his wife to me."

A way was opened. With his wife in his arms, Fortunato came before Teresita. She stood quietly, her face glowing with warmth and concern.

"I knew you were coming. Place her there," she said, pointing to a chair. Teresita took the puzzled woman's hands and gazed into her eyes for several minutes. Then she released Mariana's hands and deftly stroked the woman's hips and legs.

"Stand up," she said.

The woman, now under hypnosis, awkwardly did as she was directed.

"Walk," said Teresita gently, taking the woman's arm to guide her. Mariana walked, making several rounds, with Teresita's help, up and down the veranda.

"See, you can walk. You do not need me to help, you know." The patient hesitated, then walked the veranda by herself.

Released from hypnosis, the woman slowly realized that the use of her legs had been restored to her. Tears of gratitude filled her eyes and ran down her cheeks. Then she sank to her knees before the girl, and taking one of Teresita's hands, kissed it repeatedly. "Blessed Teresa," she sobbed, "you have made me well again. We are now your servants. My husband and I will serve you all the days of our lives. We made this promise to each other before we left our home."

"I knew you were coming to me, Mariana, and I welcome you," Teresita said as she raised the woman to her feet. An ecstatic wave of adulation swept through the crowd.

"Miracle! Miracle!" The cry carried over the walls of the compound to the people beyond.

Although given during emotional stress, Mariana's promise

was not an empty one. She was to become Teresita's friend, maid, assistant, counselor and life-long companion. Fortunato, a silver craftsman, was to forsake his trade and also be made a trusted member of Teresita's family as long as he lived.

Eventually the ever-growing throng disrupted the routine of the Urrea household completely. No corner of the premises offered any escape from the deluge of patients and curiosity seekers. People crowded onto the veranda, into the bedrooms, the warehouse and the blacksmith shop. Incensed at this invasion of his property, Don Tomás watched the spectacle in angry frustration.

Many of the uninvited guests had traveled long distances without food. Even though he abhorred their intrusion, Don Tomás could not bear to see hungry people grow hungrier. Gruffly he directed Marcos to have the vaqueros kill a beef, butcher the meat into small portions, sell the cuts to those who could pay and give them to the ones who could not. The charity cases, Don Tomás discovered, far outnumbered those with a few coins in their purse. When that beef was gone, another was butchered, and then another. Soon the *patrón* found himself feeding a populace many times the size of Cabora's. To make matters worse, most of the visitors arrived on horseback or in oxcarts, sometimes accompanied by beasts of burden carrying food, water and wares to sell along the route. The various burros, horses, mules and oxen consumed the grass of Cabora in ever-increasing amounts, making it imperative for Don Tomás to reduce his own livestock operation.

Teresita herself was becoming a source of anxiety and concern. Don Tomás worried about the strain inflicted on her fragile body and sensitive nervous system, since some of those seeking miraculous cures knew no moderation. He worried that hysterical seekers of the supernatural might force their way into her bedroom at night. To forestall such a possibility, he moved her into his own room, the one with the thick rock walls, and installed a door connecting it with the tower. Don Tomás moved into the room above, which also offered access to the tower, so that he would always be within earshot.

As the crowds grew larger, Don Tomás's worries kept pace. In a few months all the steer cattle on the Cabora range would be consumed. To protect the cows and heifers from desperate poachers, he began transferring livestock to the other ranches. In time he would have to import steers from his other holdings to feed the hungry hordes at Cabora. If something could not be done to stem the devastating waves of pilgrims, the ranch would face economic ruin. He was ever mindful of Doña Loreto's joint ownership of Cabora and realized that it was his child, not hers, who was causing the mass hysteria, leading to eventual destruction and loss. *El patrón* found himself swept along by powers beyond his command. In a land where life was based on the macho principle, Don Tomás had lost control of both his daughter and his property. This was the cruelest blow of all.

He spent his days thinking of ways to halt the onslaught of trespassers, and even stationed his vaqueros along the roads leading to the ranch with instructions to turn back all intruders. This accomplished nothing. It would have taken a thousand well-armed men to patrol the boundaries of Cabora.

Each day Don Tomás tried to convince Teresita that she should go away, offering all manner of inducements. He proposed sending her to school in the United States or France and dwelt eloquently on the advantages and satisfactions to be derived from an extensive education. In the finishing schools and universities, she would meet people of refinement and social standing. With her beauty and personality she could make a splendid marriage. His arguments seemed to amuse Teresita. Sure that he was making some headway, Don Tomás enlarged on the idea. He would give her the biggest and most glamorous wedding ever performed in Alamos. Her reply reduced his dreams to dust.

"Yes, Papá, I do intend to marry some day, but when I do, it will be a simple, quiet affair. That will not be until I have completed my commitment to the Blessed Virgin. When I do marry," she added mischievously, "people will no longer consider me a saint, and that will make you happy."

Trying another approach, Don Tomás offered to take her to Paris, outfit her in fine clothes, show her wonderful cathedrals and the greatest art galleries in the world. Then, proudly flourishing his trump card, he promised a visit to the holy shrine at Lourdes. But no matter how hard he pressed the point, she remained adamant against any plan that would separate her from the people who needed her.

After each clash of wills, Don Tomás became more upset and vehement. A traumatic confrontation seemed imminent. It came at last, and Lauro Aguirre later described the scene:

Don Tomás argued long and heatedly with Teresita, trying to get her to see the entirety of what was happening at Cabora in the context of science and reason. All this moved her not at all. The steady gaze of her large, mystical and hypnotic eyes, the quiet, tolerant expression of her countenance, the soft, arresting tone of her voice, and the simple recitation of the good she was doing, and the joy and hope she was bringing to the hundreds of poor people every day, all this disarmed him and left him more frustrated than ever.

He would retire to nurse his discontent and build up another head of counter-reaction. It is said that the dividing line between hatred and love is invisible when those one dearly loves are involved. The accumulated frustration and agitation finally pushed Don Tomás beyond the limits of sanity.

One night, after a furious argument, he grabbed Teresita by the shoulders and shook her violently with all his strength. She did not resist him. When his fury cooled he found she was regarding him with a pity and tolerance he could not endure. He let her go and abruptly climbed the stairs to the room above.

She undressed, put on her nightgown, let down her hair, brushed it slowly and lay down on the bed. She could hear her father walking back and forth. Hour after hour she listened to his pacing, and she knew that the ultimate showdown would soon come. She did not close her eyes. With her acute sensitivity, she could not only "see" her father, she could "read" his thoughts. It was as if she were in his room and he were thinking aloud. The tempo of footsteps indicated the rise and lulls in his agitation. She knew every argument, every point of view, every consideration, every quirk and turn in his chain of thoughts.

About three o'clock in the morning she was sure that the crisis was at hand. Her father was reaching the breaking point, and she knew the instant that it was reached. She lighted the candle by the bed and stood waiting. She listened to his steps descending the stairs.

The door was flung open and there he stood with a fanatical and dazed glare in his eyes, his pistol in his hand. She stood in her white nightgown, her dark hair framing an angelic countenance. She was not afraid, nor disturbed, nor angry. Her hypnotic eyes returned his wild stare.

Softly she said, "Go ahead and shoot me, papá. I will pray for you in heaven!"

Don Tomás was transfixed by the same indefinable quality he had seen affect her half-brothers when they chided her beyond endurance. He could not bring himself to raise his arm. He lowered his gaze, his head bent forward, his shoulders slumped, and the pistol dropped from his hand. Teresita moved to him, put her arms about him, led him to a chair, and gently pushed him down. Don Tomás was without words. Teresita knew the battle of wills was over. She picked up the pistol and offered it to him, handle first. Vacantly he looked at it and slowly replaced it in the holster attached to his belt. Teresita then led him back to his room.

The next day Don Tomás was a changed and chastened man. At last, he had accepted the inevitable. For the first time in months, he was at peace with himself. The strained, deepened lines of his face had softened. His hard and authoritative voice had modified. His mien had altered from that of a dominating father to one of a partner. From that day to the end of his life his fate was irretrievably linked with that of his gifted daughter.

Don Tomás's reconciliation with Teresita was complete and lasting. The Mexican historian Mario Gill interprets the *patrón*'s change in attitude toward Teresita's pursuits as a "conversion to her cause and religious concepts." However, Don Tomás never altered his views regarding natural phenomena. He continued to believe that occurrences that appeared to be supernatural were natural happenings caused by natural laws not yet discovered by man. To him the great mystery lay not in the events, but in the Creator who made the laws that produced and controlled the events.

His change of attitude was motivated primarily by his paternal love for his daughter, a love verging on obsession, and secondarily by the good work she was accomplishing. From that night on, Teresita and her ministrations took priority over everything at Cabora. Don Tomás energetically set about improving the conditions for her work, giving her the house of one of the *mayordomos* a short distance from the Casa Grande. The house featured broad portals on either side, where Teresita could receive her patients. After the place was entirely reconditioned and whitewashed, he installed her there with a small staff of assistants and servants. Henceforth it was called Teresita's house.

Josefina Félix was there much of the time as a companion and assistant. Mariana Avendano acted as both housekeeper and assistant; her husband, Fortunato, became the servant of all work, providing wood, water and provisions, and running all sorts of errands. Don Tomás placed much stress on their guarding Teresita's bedroom against intruders at all times.

With Teresita's removal to her own premises, a considerable degree of order and privacy was restored to the Casa Grande. The reconciliation with his daughter also gave Don Tomás greater peace of mind, allowing him to devote more time to managing the cattle on all the ranches, overseeing the farms and crops, and attending the business of feeding the pilgrims. By careful supervision of the distribution of meat and *masa* (a dough for making cornmeal tortillas) and by charging those who had money enough to pay for those without any, he managed the economy of the ranches on a break-even basis.

Chapter Nine

MANUEL MENDOZA, the newspaper reporter cited in the prologue, was an eyewitness to the events of a typical day at Cabora in the summer of 1891. The story of his visit has been handed down through Henry Aguirre, Don Lauro's son, who first heard it when he was a young man in his twenties. Retold many times, his version no doubt has been tightened, polished and dramatized; yet the substance rings true. The following is Henry Aguirre's account of what a skeptical, hardheaded newspaper man observed on the occasion of that unforgettable visit.

Mendoza rode south on the dust-filled road from Cajame toward Navojoa. Soon he came to an intersection with another road. Where the roads crossed, a shrewd peasant woman had built a ramada under which she operated a *tienda*, a roadside stand offering simple foods and refreshments for sale. The reporter turned in to the stand to ask directions. From the number of people he had passed during the morning, he judged the woman was reaping a goodly profit.

"Can you tell me the way to Cabora?" he asked.

The woman stared at him as though unable to believe that anyone in this world could fail to know the way to Cabora.

"It is that way, sir," she said, pointing east. "Everyone goes there."

The reporter got off his sweaty horse, bought some refreshments, and stood in the shade, mopping his forehead with a linen handkerchief. The sky was blue and cloudless, and the summer sun was beating fiercely. The man finished his meager repast and stood watching the people coming and going past the crossroads.

One fairly large group, evidently a humble family of laborers, must have come from afar, judging by their road-weary appearance. A man walked in front of the group, holding aloft a cross made of two tree branches. From the horizontal limb waved a white banner, upon which, in crude red letters, was inscribed "La Santa de Cabora." Behind him walked two barefoot women carrying a child on a small litter. The group paused in front of the refreshment stand, its members looking wistfully at the wares. Then they passed a gourd canteen of water among themselves and continued on the road to Cabora.

The reporter drew a notebook from the pocket of his shirt and made entries as the *tienda* owner watched suspiciously. Before he had finished writing, he heard singing. Glancing up, he saw a group coming along the road from Navojoa. It too was made up of working people, but they were better fed and dressed, and they walked with more spring to their steps. The leader was singing and the others joined in on the choruses. At the rear of the party, a blind man walked with the cautious pace of the sightless, holding onto a woman's shoulder with one gnarled hand. At the stand the singing ceased, the members of the group conferred, the leader took up a collection, and with the copper coins in his hand, he came to the *tienda* woman and bargained for cactus candy. The haggling finished and the sweets distributed, the party resumed their march toward Cabora.

While the reporter was still making notes, a large collection of people arrived along the road from Cabora. The returning pilgrims were in good spirits. One man strummed a guitar as he walked, furnishing the accompaniment for several joyous singers. Mendoza noted that there were no sick or blind among them.

J. CISNEROS

The party stopped at the stand, where a few made purchases as the others stood by, looking longingly at the items for sale.

Hearing the distant, plaintive notes of a primitive flute, Mendoza looked up expectantly in the direction of Cajame. Two *pascola* dancers came in sight, leading a party of thirty or forty Indians. The dancers in the group were barefoot and naked except for blanket breech-clouts, wooden masks hanging on one side of their heads, and dried cocoon rattles circling their ankles. In their hands they carried round gourd rattles. They walked several paces with light, springy steps and danced a few measures ending in graceful whirls, all the while rhythmically shaking the gourd rattles. Repeating their walking-dancing movements, they continued down the road. The men immediately following the dancers were all heavily armed. Each carried a Winchester rifle swung by a leather thong across his back, two cartridge belts over the chest, and a vicious-looking knife stuck in his belt. At the rear of the party, four tall, strong warriors carried a man on a litter. When the group came closer, the reporter heard the *tienda* woman's respectful whisper, "Yaquis." The group kept to the road, passing the refreshment stand. Its customers gave them a wide berth, studiously ignoring their fierce and rhythmic dance. Intensely involved in their procession, the Indians filled the road as if they were the only people in the world. Mendoza wrote furiously in his book.

Then he noticed a ragged man with a barrel-organ, who had appeared from somewhere and was grinding out a tune. On the edge of the organ perched a parrot that screeched angrily whenever the instrument hit certain notes, amusing both Mendoza and the crowd, some of whom pitched copper coins into the musician's cup.

The reporter watched the various groups come and go, most of them traveling on foot. A few rode burros, mules or horses. One bullcart with solid wooden wheels creaked by, its driver walking beside the oxen. Inside the cart, a pallid old man lay on a bed of straw, stoically ignoring the bumps as the vehicle clattered along the uneven road. Some of the pilgrims were provided with all that was necessary to their comfort during such a journey. Others carried only small bundles on their backs, and a few apparently had nothing at all. All of these observations the reporter diligently recorded.

Mendoza noticed that many pilgrims wore *escapularios*. He recalled having seen them once before in a San Juan's day procession at the mission of Tubac in Arizona. They were made of two small, rectangular pieces of thick cloth, each about six by eight inches, one worn on the chest and one on the back, the two supported by ribbons passing over the shoulders. The front cloth was embroidered in Spanish with the words "Hail, Blessed Teresita," and the back rectangle carried the message, also in Spanish, "The Great Power of God Rules the World." Many of the pilgrims carried sheets of paper, like handbills, each with a badly printed text.

"What is that?" he asked a field worker who held one such paper.

"A prayer."

"Can you read it?" Mendoza asked.

"No."

"May I see it?" The man handed the sheet to him. It was a simple prayer in Spanish addressed to "Blessed Teresita," the "Saint of Cabora," asking her to intercede with the Holy Mother on behalf of the bearer.

Mendoza made a final entry in his notebook and then snapped it closed and returned the book to his shirt pocket. He took off his hat, again mopping the sweat from his eyes and forehead. The *tienda* woman looked at him inquiringly. "Is there something wrong, sir?"

The reporter gave her an indulgent smile. "Not with me, Señora."

Mendoza handed her a coin and was preparing to mount his horse when a carriage arrived from the north, rattling noisily along the road. In the back seat were a well-dressed man and boy. After the carriage stopped, the man got out. The reporter saw that he was tall, lean and vigorous. The *tienda* woman regarded his flashing and expressive eyes admiringly while he purchased lemonade for the boy, the driver and himself. As he paid the woman, he noticed Mendoza watching him.

"Won't you drink with us?" he asked.

"With pleasure," said the reporter, professionally curious as to the traveler's identity and the nature of his mission. He found the stranger easy to converse with, and the two chatted agreeably as they finished their lemonade.

"Where are you going?" Mendoza ventured.

"To Cabora."

"So am I."

"Then won't you ride with us? We can lead your horse behind the carriage."

"I will if it does not crowd you."

"Not at all. Please enter."

Once in the carriage the tall man said, "Let us introduce ourselves. I am Luís Alamán, and this is my nephew, Carlos."

"My name is Manuel Mendoza. I am with the Arizona *Daily Star* in Tucson."

"You are going to interview La Santa?"

"Yes, señor." The reporter noticed that the boy regarded him with a steady stare.

"Why are you going to Cabora, Carlos?" The boy said nothing, but continued to stare at him.

"Forgive him. He cannot hear you," his uncle explained. "He is deaf and dumb."

"Then you are taking him to be cured?"

"Yes."

The reporter seemed surprised that a person of Luís's station should be on such a mission.

"Tell me," he asked, "do you believe that she can cure him?"

"No."

"If you lack faith, then I don't understand why you are going."

"It is to please my mother," the man sighed. "She has much faith."

"Has the boy always been like this?"

"No. Until two years ago he was perfectly normal. Then he was involved in an accident."

The reporter felt an urge to draw his notebook from his pocket but stopped himself. "Would you mind telling me about the accident?"

Luís explained how his nephew, his sister's only child, had suffered a horrible emotional shock. The carriage in which the boy and his parents were riding was attacked by bandits, and Carlos saw his father and mother brutally murdered. The bandits struck the child on the head and left him for dead. Physically, he had recovered, but the shock of the tragedy was so terrible that he had not spoken since, and was apparently stone-deaf. Luís's mother had heard of the so-called cures of the "Saint of Cabora" and had persuaded him to bring the boy. His mother was ill and could not make the trip herself.

The afternoon shadows were long when the Alamán carriage approached Cabora. A mile from the ranch headquarters the travelers began to pass the encampments of pilgrims. Shelters of every kind—tents, lean-tos made of brush, enclosures of carrizo cane mats—stood haphazardly assembled a few yards from the road. As the carriage drew near the ranch buildings, the driver had to stop frequently because so many people filled the path. When the vehicle could go no farther, the reporter, followed by Luís holding Carlos by the hand, pushed his way on foot into the dense crowd gathered before what he assumed to be Teresita's house. The going was slow, but they came at last to a spot from which they could see a girl, who without doubt was Teresa Urrea. In front of her were two men supporting a crippled woman. Teresita placed her hand on the woman's forehead and talked to her in a low murmur. Mendoza then heard Teresita's voice, carrying clearly as she addressed the men holding the woman. "Let her stand alone."

With obvious reluctance, the men released their charge, who remained upright. She looked around uncertainly as if she could not believe she was actually standing without support. The two men were visibly shaken. One of the bystanders shouted, "Miracle!" and others repeated the word until its sound spread to the very edges of the crowd. People stood on tiptoe and craned their necks to catch a glimpse of the fortunate woman. A pathway opened as the men led the former patient, now walking without help, through the crowd.

In the commotion, Mendoza, Luís and Carlos found themselves pushed so close to Teresita that they could almost touch her. Intent on her ministrations, she took no notice of them. A stretcher was now placed in front of her, holding an old man, seriously ill, gaunt and emaciated. Teresita knelt beside the stretcher and caressed the old man's withered hand. She spoke to him softly, her voice plainly audible in the silence that had settled over the throng.

"It is Our Lord's wish that you live in suffering, but He will give you the strength to bear it. Just now He is very near your body. Open your heart wide so that He may enter, because soon you will be in God's presence. Think only of that instant, and prepare your soul for that day, which will be a glorious one for you. Look toward Heaven, for that will be your abode." Teresita rose and, lifting her hands, addressed the multitude: "Let us each pray that this man will find relief from his affliction."

All of the women and a few of the men knelt. Most of the men remained standing, as did the reporter and Luís, removing their wide-brimmed hats.

Teresita lifted her face and her lips moved silently. As he scrutinized her, Mendoza thought he detected a slight difference in the two sides of Teresita's face. One seemed to be more sensual, the other more spiritual. Captivated by the mere sight of the woman, his thoughts raced on in silent appraisal: "Not a classic beauty. Loveliness rather than beauty. What she has transcends beauty. It is something that projects. Projects and disarms. . . . A warmth, a glow, eagerness and sincerity, a magnetism. Eyes that inspire confidence and faith, that probe and hypnotize. An arresting and remarkable woman. With the unconscious talent of a great actress, she establishes a spellbinding rapport with her audience. It is clear why believers find her irresistible. She tells them to walk and they walk. But for all her saintliness and good works, she is still a woman, a sensually attractive woman. . . . Just now she is tired, depleted and overworked, nearing exhaustion."

When Teresita had finished her prayer and opened her eyes, she looked down at young Carlos. The boy had not taken his gaze from her since he first saw her. Noticing his intense interest, she smiled. He responded shyly. Only a few inches behind him, Mendoza watched the silent interchange, then shifted his attention to the patients on the porch.

The son of the old man on the stretcher knelt beside him and exclaimed, dismayed, "She did not cure you, father!"

"She has done something better, my son. She has given me peace. Now take me home." The four men lifted the stretcher and pushed their way through the crowd, which opened a little and closed again as soon as the small group had passed.

A woman with a child limp in her arms hurried toward Teresita, who gave her a look of encouragement. Teresita began to raise the rebozo covering the child, then swayed unsteadily, seemingly overcome by dizziness. She put her hand to her forehead, covering her eyes, as she wavered back and forth. She was on the verge of collapse when Luís stepped forward and took hold of her. Then she fainted completely.

Mariana came running anxiously, and pointed toward the door of Teresita's bedroom. Luís lifted her easily and carried her inside, placing her on the bed. After the reporter and Carlos had followed Luís into the house, Mariana sent a servant to fetch Don Tomás and then firmly closed the front door. Mendoza was alert, determined not to miss any part of such a unique opportunity. He noticed that Carlos hovered near the bedroom door, looking with distress at Teresita, and that Luís stood to one side of the bed and a little back, eyes fastened on the "saintly" side of the woman's face. Mariana patted a cloth dampened with balm water over Teresita's pale forehead. Then Mendoza saw the girl open her eyes and silently regard Luís for the first time.

Teresita was still looking at Luís when Don Tomás rushed into the room. She shifted her gaze to her father and smiled wanly. His relief in finding she was only in a swoon was apparent to Mendoza. To cover up his discomposure in front of strangers, the *patrón* said gruffly, "*Niña mía,* you must not try to see so many people in one day. You are exhausting yourself. You should use better judgment."

The next day, the boy and the two men were invited to return to the house. Mendoza stood inconspicuously in a corner of Teresita's living room, observing. Carlos was seated on a chair and standing beside him were Luís Alamán and Don Tomás. Facing the boy, on a low stool, was Teresita. The reporter concentrated on Carlos's reaction to Teresita and felt he could interpret the boy's thoughts.

This was the bewitching woman who had smiled at him yesterday. Her kindly, magnetic eyes seemed to be penetrating deep into him. The compassionate radiance of her face gripped and held him . . . the most compelling, the most beautiful face he had ever seen. He wished he could reach out and touch her cheek, but he could not raise his hand. He was helpless. This marvelous woman had him in her power. His will was not his own. She controlled him. Anything to please her. Anything. He saw her lips moving but could hear nothing. Still she held him. His concentration was very great. He thought he could read her lips. She seemed to be saying, "You can hear, Carlos. You can hear. You must forget what happened. Forget, Carlos, forget.

The expressions passing over the boy's face mirrored what he was reliving at that moment.

Forget? From afar he heard it again. A sound like rolling stones, big ones going down a mountain very fast. The crescendo became deafening. The assault on the carriage, the horses rearing on their hind feet when the bandits jumped out from hiding, the terror on his mother's face as she was jerked from the carriage, his father's springing at the bandits, the shot, and his father's body slumping beside the road, the screams of his mother, their dragging her to the brush nearby, her last agonized moan, a bandit striking him with a gun barrel.

Mendoza saw Carlos shiver from head to foot. Even had he wished, the boy could not take his gaze from the beautiful lady. His concentration was riveted on her moving lips.

"You can hear, Carlos, you can hear. . . ."

He now appeared to hear, as though listening to sounds coming from a vast distance. Or was it an illusion? The reporter saw Carlos shut his eyes so that he could not see the lips moving. He still appeared to hear, though straining with every muscle in his small body.

"You can hear, Carlos. Forget. Forget. Speak, speak to me. You can talk, Carlos," Teresita said.

Now Mendoza was sure the boy could hear. The lovely voice must be penetrating, louder, nearer. Carlos opened his eyes and looked again at the woman. A smile of triumph came to his lips. He seemed to want very much to please her.

"I can hear you." He spoke haltingly.

"Tell me your name," Teresita urged.

"Carlos." His voice was awkward.

Mendoza, as well as the boy, witnessed the expression of rejoicing that lighted the face of the radiant young woman. Her eyes filled with tears, and a sweet fragrance filled the room. She must appear like an angel to the boy, Mendoza thought. He heard Luís utter a sob and looking up, saw that great beads of sweat stood on the tall man's forehead as he stood transfixed. The reporter became conscious of his own incredulous state of mind, as the boy's radiant eyes fastened on him.

"I saw it happen with my own eyes . . . but I still can't believe it!" Mendoza thought to himself.

The reporter next looked at the *patrón* of the ranch. Don Tomás was regarding the boy with utter amazement.

The boy turned to Luís. "I can talk now, Uncle Luís."

Luís Alamán, in his gratitude, was not ashamed of his tears.

Chapter Ten

As THE YEAR 1891 drew to a close, the activity at Cabora became ever more frenetic. The ranch and its immediate environs began to resemble a goldrush boomtown, with a population that swelled to bursting almost overnight. Most of the pilgrims stayed only a day or two and left as soon as their ailments were treated, their curiosity satisfied, or their religious fervor rewarded with a glimpse of Teresita. A relatively small minority came and stayed for profit, even when that profit meant only a few centavos. This group included vendors, gamblers, beggars, prostitutes and quacks of all kinds. They were wanderers who drifted from place to place, anywhere crowds of people congregated. Now they flocked to Cabora to ply their trades, their tricks and their professions. Some were honest, selling wares of their own making. Others hawked stolen objects. Gamblers dealt in games of chance, readily fleecing one another when given the opportunity.

Many of the honest tradesmen traveled long distances, carrying goods on their backs or on burros. Makers of pottery walked from as far as Guadalajara, six hundred miles away, lugging crates heavier and almost as large as themselves, the load supported by straps across their foreheads. Day after day, they jogged up and down mountain roads and across the plains, subsisting on parched corn and sleeping on the ground beside the road. Pottery was one commodity used by everyone in Mexico. Since it was fragile and easily broken, there was always a market, though the profits were small. After selling his wares and returning home, each vendor could reckon his wages at a few centavos per day.

The individual tradespeople were all highly specialized. One sold brightly colored handkerchiefs, another hand-woven rebozos, another leather belts or huaraches, ropes, hat bands, straw hats, rosaries, necklaces, *chicle* (chewing gum) and so on. Each of these itinerant hawkers carried his or her entire stock. A seller of hats, for instance, carried a stack of hats of different sizes atop his own head. None had stalls, booths or fixed places of exchange, except for the women offering food, who usually sat flat on the ground in the shade of a serape stretched over the limb of a tree or supported by sticks. One woman would sell strong, thick, pungent coffee from an earthen pot on a bed of coals, dispensing cupfuls of the brew from a single clay mug. Others peddled beans in pots, or tortillas cooked over coal fires. Beverages for sale included diluted fruit juices and the inevitable shots of watered-down mezcal, dispensed from jugs.

Numerous hawkers sold *escapularios* with various embroidered inscriptions: "La Santa de Cabora," "Santa Teresa" and "Blessed Teresa." A ready market could also be found for prayer sheets or banners decorated with prayers to Teresita. At the outer edges of the crowd were those who lived by their wits: the gamblers and swindlers, armed with dice or cards, eager to engage unwary visitors in games of chance. Professional athletes played *vencidos* with the young men, easily relieving the uninitiated of their few centavos. Equally clever promoters of cockfights and horse races found willing dupes for rigged matches. The most innocent diversions included the performances of organ grinders accompanied by parrots or monkeys, amusing the crowds for the few chance coins tossed their way. Musicians strolled about with guitars and homemade violins, singing ballads.

The most colorful performances were the religious dances

of the Yaqui Indians. There was the deer dancer, who performed with a small deer head attached to the top of his own head, imitating the movements of a deer with breathtaking accuracy. The *pascolas,* always in pairs and both wearing masks, performed their rhythmic stomping dance. Most spectacular of all were the *matachines,* a dozen or more, who did a swinging, whirling dance with colorful *coronas* on their heads, keeping time with gourd rattles and brilliant feather wands. All the dances were solemn, dignified and impressive. None of the participants asked for or accepted pay. The performances were serious, dedicated supplications to the newly adopted saint of the Yaquis, La Santa de Cabora.

Although constantly occupied with patients and confined to her new quarters, Teresita was well aware of all the hubbub around Cabora and wished that she might have the pleasure of mixing with the crowds. Good sense, however, compelled her to realize that she would be surrounded instantly and mobbed by well-wishers and supplicants.

Many of the visitors to Cabora hoped to talk with Teresita about religion. The vast majority who witnessed her feats of healing, without stint and without pay, were convinced that she was a highly religious person. Lauro Aguirre, a dedicatedly religious man himself, believed that she was deeply religious, but in a very special and unusual way. Born and reared in a community where every child was baptized a Roman Catholic, Teresita received her early religious training totally within the framework of that faith. However, Lauro perceived that her close relationship with her father, a Mason and a freethinker, and with Aguirre himself, a devout Protestant, had caused her religious convictions to become considerably modified.

Her precepts were as simple as the Ten Commandments or the Sermon on the Mount. For Teresita, the essence of religion was love: love of God and love of one's fellow man. If everyone truly loved his fellow man—all men—there would be no war, no poverty and no injustice. No priest, no organization, no authority was necessary to intervene between man and God.

In his biography of Teresita, Aguirre summed up her faith: "Her code was simple and candid. She did not believe in external trappings, the wearing of vestments, the endless muttering of prayers with little meaning for people, the constant ritual recited by rote, or palatial church buildings with gilded altars. To her, religion was a force within a person, an attitude, something that had a direct relation with God. She believed in prayer. To her, praying was like talking to a revered friend, one in whom she felt the utmost trust. Prayers should be offered with profound feeling, should be soul-stirring and heartfelt. She objected to the prayers of priests—empty, external, impersonal, without feeling; memorized passages, alike for all persons and all occasions. A parrot could perform as well."

No evidence exists that Teresita ever criticized the Roman Catholic Church. She did not approve of the conduct of those comfort-loving priests who extracted money from the poor to gratify their own appetites, and on this subject she was passionately outspoken.

Among the visitors to Cabora was a priest of just such dubious repute, a man named Manuel Gustelúm from Uruachic in the sierras of Chihuahua. Father Gustelúm had come to Cabora to collect evidence that Teresita was not a saint, that she was instead a fake and a heretic, bent on usurping the prerogatives of the ordained priesthood.

Teresita, quickly sensing a hostile person in the crowd, spotted the priest, but she gave no evidence of her awareness. The padre took note of a number of transgressions. He saw people kneel and kiss her hand, an act that should be performed for no lesser a personage than a bishop. What enraged him most was the adoration and veneration Teresita inspired in these people. She held them under some magnetic spell, an effect that could only be produced by Satan himself.

As he watched, Teresita abruptly became silent and motionless. He heard people around him whisper, "A trance, a trance. There will be a revelation." Almost immediately, a man and a woman appeared and, supporting Teresita by the arms, led her into the house. Irritated by her sudden disappearance, the priest turned and pushed his way through the crowd. At its edge he came upon two nuns, whom he had never seen before. An idea occurred to him.

Father Gustelúm was a huge man with a domineering manner and a commanding voice. To the nuns he said, "Sisters, they say La Santa is in a trance and will receive a revelation. Let us test her and see if she is sincere or only faking." Noticing a hat pin in the headdress of one of the nuns, he pulled it out.

"Take this," he said. "Go into her room. If she is in a trance, stick it through the calf of her leg. See if she flinches."

The nuns were aghast and stood staring at him, one of them gingerly holding the hat pin as if it were poisoned. Harshly, the priest commanded, "Go. Do what you are told." The nuns dared not disobey him.

When they entered her room, Teresita was resting on her bed, her eyes open and staring at the ceiling. Mariana gave them a friendly nod and said, "It is not serious. I must go to the big house for a moment. Stay if you wish." She smiled and left the room.

Quickly the older nun went to the bed and touched Teresita's shoulder. She gave no response. Lifting the girl's skirt, she thrust the hat pin through the calf of her leg. It went in easily, the point protruding slightly on the other side of the slender leg. The girl did not flinch. Becoming distraught, the nun tried to withdraw the pin. She could not budge it. Using both hands, she tried again with all her strength. The pin remained fast. The nuns looked at each other in anguish, not knowing what to do next. They started backing away toward the door. Teresita suddenly came out of her trance, reached down and withdrew the long hat pin without effort. No blood came from the wound.

The nuns stood by the door, frozen and horrified by their deed. Quietly the girl said, "Take this back to the priest who sent you and tell him what you have seen."

The two women rushed to the bed, fell on their knees, and one after the other kissed Teresita's hand. "Forgive us, Our Lady, we have done a terrible thing and have witnessed a miracle. Now we believe!"

In a consoling voice she replied, "I do not perform miracles. Only God can do that."

Teresita's trances had become so frequent that the family considered them a routine occurrence. Several might occur in a single day, or else days might pass before Teresita again received a revelation during such periods of semi-consciousness. The revelations might be happy in content, pertaining to the birth of a baby, the arrival of a cherished friend, a much-needed rain at some distant place or other pleasing communications. Or they might be tragic in nature, disclosing the death of a relative or friend, an accident, an earthquake, a volcanic eruption or some similar disaster. When such pronouncements became known to the illiterate masses who made up the vast majority of pilgrims, and when subsequent events proved the predictions to be correct, they were hailed as "miracles."

Antonio Félix, brother of Josefina Félix, described another type of psychic experience Teresita could induce for no purpose other than to entertain her closest friends. She could take them instantly, or leisurely, to distant places through the air. The experience would be so realistic and vivid that the companion afterwards believed he or she actually had been wafted physically through the air in a journey to some new locale.

As we know, Josefina and Teresita spent much time visiting each other and often spent the night together. One evening, after a strenuous day at Baroyeca, the two were resting in bed, tired and spent. "Josefina," Teresita asked, "how would you like to take a trip to Mexico City?"

"Very much," her friend answered.

"Then take my hand," Teresita said to her smilingly.

Josefina later described to her family her strange experience. No doubt Teresita cast a hypnotic spell, but as Josefina told it, everything she experienced was real. They went flying through the air over mountains, forests and deserts to Mexico City, where they descended and strolled along the streets and through leafy parks. They saw avenues filled with elegant horse-drawn carriages, fashionably dressed people and countless other sights of the great city they had never visited before. Next, they flew over Xochilmilco and saw the "Floating Gardens." Finally they took a swoop over the Pyramids of the Sun and Moon at Teotihuacán. Returning by a different route, they found themselves in bed again, delightfully tired.

Antonio Alvarado recalled an occasion when Teresita escorted another girl on such a trip, while Josefina consciously stood witness to the experience. She observed that Teresita and her friend became rigid and appeared comatose. When the spell was over, the companion emerged from the imaginary journey with total recall of all she had seen.

About this time, Josefina also had occasion to observe Teresita's ability to "see things at a distance." Josefina's married sister in Baroyeca was expecting a baby. Around two o'clock one morning Teresita awakened Josefina and told her gleefully, "You have a fine, healthy niece in Baroyeca. She weighs four kilos."

"How do you know?"

"I was there and helped with the delivery."

"When?"

"Just now, a few minutes ago."

Josefina was so accustomed to her friend's feats that she did not even question the assertion. The next day they learned that the baby had arrived just as Teresita had reported. The mother said that Teresita was with her and the birth was painless.

Stories of this type were told and retold with various embellishments. Many people fervently believed that Teresita could transport herself through the air physically and instantaneously.

Ignacio Paredes and his sister Elena of Sinaloa were frequent visitors at Cabora. They were cousins of Doña Loreto; nevertheless, they were completely devoted to Teresita. While staying at Cabora, they became members of her staff, assisting her in every way possible. As serious practitioners of spiritualism, both were keenly interested in Teresita's extrasensory powers. They spent much time in the evenings explaining the mysteries of the séance and holding their own communions with the dead. Spiritualism was nothing new to Teresita, who had listened often to Lauro Aguirre and her father discussing the phenomenon at length. She was tolerant of the views held by Ignacio and Elena and no doubt cooperated in their séances, but there is no evidence, either written or oral, that Teresita herself was a spiritualist.

Teresita was venerated by the masses in Mexico as a healer, and soon her reputation for extrasensory powers attracted attention in scientific circles throughout the United States, Europe and Asia. Physicians came from abroad to study her techniques and determine the nature of her cures. Students and followers of the occult, including a group of Brahmins from India, arrived to observe her extrasensory gifts. According to Valades, she cooperated with all visitors of serious intent.

Chapter Eleven

Outside the peaceful and often festive world of Cabora, the Díaz regime was making life difficult, even perilous, for many in Mexico. Teresita, occupied day and night with visitors and patients, was oblivious to the political rumblings, but Don Tomás knew well enough what was afoot and grew anxious over the dictator's increasingly oppressive government.

During his second term of office, Porfirio Díaz tightened his control over all of Mexico. Political rivals and malcontents were silenced through brutal object lessons. General García de la Cadena was murdered when reports of his plots for a revolt in Zacatecas reached the ears of Díaz. A dozen other opposition leaders were assassinated under strange and diverse circumstances. No assassin was brought to justice for any of these or other political murders.

Effective instruments of the dictatorship were the corrupt state governors. As a reward for their loyalty to the Díaz government, they were free to terrorize at will, murdering political opponents and thereby becoming the owners of large haciendas and commercial monopolies. The reform movement initiated under Díaz by Benito Juárez, instead of destroying the old feudalism, ended in creating a new one. Mestizos who were formerly generals in the War of Reform were now *hacendados* secure in the political hierarchy. Half Spanish and half Mixtec Indian, Díaz himself belonged to this class.

After the dictator gained control of the state administrations, elections to the national congress became a mere formality. Díaz compiled lists of people he wanted in congress and sent the names to the governors, who distributed them to local officials, the governor's appointees. Sometimes mistakes occurred when the lists contained names of deceased constituents. It mattered little if the dead were elected to congress, however. Had they been alive the congressional vote would still have been directed by the dictator.

The lower court magistrates were appointed by the supreme court, the judges of the supreme court were appointed by congress, and congress was selected by Díaz, thus giving the dictator complete control of the judiciary. Under Díaz, foreigners, especially Americans, received favorable verdicts. Lawsuits against Mexicans of wealth and position were determined by their loyalty to the government rather than by the facts involved. For peons, peasants and workers, justice was always on the side of power.

Ordinarily one would suppose that a dictator of iron will, devoid of pity or compassion, insensitive to human suffering, would have used every source of power for personal aggrandizement. Ironically, Díaz apparently had no desire for personal wealth. He died a relatively poor man. He never stole for himself, but he blatantly permitted his henchmen to steal half of Mexico as long as they were loyal to him.

The dictator had two consuming ambitions. One was for personal power, in quest of which he let nothing stand in his way. The other was for development of a powerful Mexico. This goal could be achieved only by developing her natural resources, a process that required foreign capital. In order to attract the necessary funds, Díaz knew that he must make Mexico a safe place for investments, while offering attractive concessions to interested foreigners.

J. CISNEROS

To promote an image of safety and security, Díaz created two strong arms of law enforcement. For the first time in Mexico's history, the army became a thoroughly disciplined organization. Any officer whose loyalty was even slightly suspect was shot. Díaz's famous *rurales* formed the other arm of the government's strategy for policing the nation. This organization was composed almost entirely of tough, hardened, unscrupulous men on the order of the North American desperadoes—Billy the Kid, Sam Bass and, later, John Dillinger and Clyde Barrow. Picturesquely garbed in broad felt hats and gray uniforms with silver buttons and red ties, the *rurales* rode the finest horses in Mexico, equipped with silver-embossed saddles. The recruits' loyalty was assured by allowing them to exercise their old habits of robbing and terrorizing the peasants. They cleverly erased all evidence of pillage by invoking the *Ley Fuga*: the custom of shooting their victims, who were then reported to have been shot while trying to escape. Outlaw banditry was replaced by legal banditry: the *rurales* were a mighty factor in guaranteeing law, order and stability for potential investors. Aided by this ruthless little band and the larger forces of the Mexican army, Díaz easily suppressed every evidence of resistance to his regime. Mexico became the safest place on earth for everyone except the unfortunate Mexicans and Indians.

Díaz also engineered a one-sided peace with the Roman Catholic Church and agreed to cease enforcing the *Ley Lerdo*— the property-confiscation law—against the Church in exchange for its support. As a warning measure, he made sure the bishops knew that the law would remain on the statute books and would be vigorously enforced at the first sign of ecclesiastical opposition to his rule. A quarter-century later, this agreement was to be the death blow for the Church in Mexico. However, throughout the Díaz regime, the Church supported his policy of "security and domestic peace." This bargain between the clergy and the dictator also added indirectly to a chain of events that ultimately affected Cabora.

When the dictator could no longer dip into the lands and properties of the Church to reward his henchmen, generals, governors and foreign investors, he had only two other resources available: public lands and the communal holdings of the Indians. As Díaz applied it to the Indian lands, the *Ley Lerdo* provided that any properties for which the pueblo or tribe did not hold documentary title were subject to confiscation by the government. The Indians of Mexico were for the most part sedentary, and their claims to their lands went back to pre-Columbian times. Because these unwritten prior titles had never been questioned, Indian rights had always been recognized by the Spanish colonial government and previous Mexican governments. The enforcement of the *Ley Lerdo* in its new application was destined to bring trouble.

In 1875, years before Teresita had begun curing the sick and afflicted, a bloody Yaqui war had broken out a short distance north of Cabora. Under the leadership of Cajame, an able Yaqui soldier who had fought under Juárez in the War of Reform, the Yaquis had retreated into the Bacatete Mountains. In defense of their tribal territory, they continued to defeat every army the government sent against them until they were temporarily subjugated by starvation. Cajame was captured and shot, but his followers were by no means defeated. It was only a matter of time, they knew, until they could regroup and fight again.

Highly religious in a pagan-Christian way, the Yaquis were an animistic people who employed the services of wizards and witches, as well as of their own priests. Given their belief in omens and oracles, they were bound to be drawn to Teresita's supernatural powers. During the short-lived respite between the death of Cajame and the next rebellion under Tetabiate, the Yaquis came to Cabora in large numbers, many to be cured, and others to seek Teresita's advice as an oracle. The chiefs, in private interviews with her, mournfully described the wrongs and injustices they had suffered at the hands of the government, and denounced Díaz's new policy of confiscating Indian lands. Believing she had influence with God, they pressed for advice and counsel.

Teresita agreed that their grievances were real, but insisted that she was only an ordinary woman, with no knowledge of political affairs or influence with the government. She admonished the Yaquis to be patient and tolerant. Explaining her doctrine of love and good will in simple parables, she advised them that love was far more effective than bullets. To the Yaqui warriors it was evident that her sympathy and compassion for their plight was great. The chiefs were mature and wise in some respects, and stubbornly childlike in others. To them Teresita was a symbol of all that was good and just. Pointedly ignoring all her demurrers, the Yaquis insisted on regarding her as a saint with God-given powers beyond the normal.

Díaz's relentless efforts to oust the Yaquis from their lands equaled those directed at the Mayo tribes, their neighbors to the south. The Mayos inhabited several hundred thousand acres of fertile coastal land, irrigated by the waters of the Río Mayo. Under the *Ley Lerdo*, these lands were rapidly being handed over to *hacendados* and irrigation companies. The Mayos, less warlike than their Yaqui neighbors, accepted their dispossession with grim stoicism. But beneath the apparent resignation to their fate lurked smoldering animosity and resentment. Like the Yaquis, the Mayos considered Teresita a genuine saint, and sent their chiefs to confer with her. She offered them the same counsel she gave to the Yaquis: their difficulties could be surmounted only through love and patient forbearance.

Meanwhile, the *Ley Lerdo* was taking its toll in the sierras to the east, where hundreds of isolated little villages nestled in the narrow river valleys. Tillable land in the region was scarce; there was only enough to grow beans, peppers, pumpkins, and corn for tortillas. Cattle were raised on the mountain sides, which were considered common lands by the villagers, and the forests of the foothills yielded only hogs of the razorback family, rooting for bulbs and tubers. The mestizos and Tarahumara Indians who lived in the villages were poor, barely able to subsist on the arid land. To the casual visitor, who could get to the villages only on foot or by muleback, they seemed to have nothing to tempt the government into invoking the *Ley Lerdo*.

However, the mountains were covered with virgin forests— tall pines and sturdy spruce—and lumber was a scarce commodity in most of Mexico. Buried deep within the mountains themselves were untapped veins of silver, gold and copper. All of these re- sources promised great wealth for the man with sufficient capital to develop the area. Inexorably the *Ley Lerdo* took effect in the sierras. The people of the villages were informed by government officials that the lands they had held for generations no longer belonged to them.

A swell of anger and frustration swept through the villages of the sierras. These mountaineers were proud, independent, superstitious and fanatically religious. Teresita's fame had pene- trated even into this remote region. In increasing numbers, in- dividuals and small groups from mountain villages made pil- grimages to Cabora. There they mingled and exchanged news with other pilgrims from villages hundreds of miles away. They returned home from Cabora with two convictions: Teresita was a saint, and opposition to the *Ley Lerdo* was widespread. Many of these pilgrims, they learned, were already dispossessed victims of the *Ley Lerdo*.

Most of the mountain-dwellers kept their thoughts to them- selves and were wary of making utterances that might be used against them. But there was no mistaking the undercurrent of discontent. It was inevitable that some of the bolder should ex- change ideas, give vent to their resentment, and air their griev- ances. Soon Cabora became a meeting ground for unhappy villagers and Indian alike. The very air buzzed with rumors of revolt.

Don Tomás was aware of the rumblings among the pilgrims and was deeply troubled by the atmosphere of rebellion. The government was similarly aware. Agents, dressed in shabby clothes and worn-out huaraches, arrived to spy on the visitors. Even among the crowd of similarly dressed pilgrims, Don Tomás knew they were there.

Chapter Twelve

IN 1890 REPORTS of the "miracles" of the Saint of Cabora reached the village of Tomochic, in the high western sierras of the state of Chihuahua.

"Tomochic" is a Tarahumara place-name meaning "The Place to Settle"; the original connotation was "a good place to settle." The village is located in a valley in the Sierra Madre Chihuahuense about thirty-five miles southwest of Ciudad Guerrero, which in turn is about a hundred twenty-five miles west of Chihuahua City. In pre-Spanish times, the village was an Indian settlement. Those who have seen the area describe it as the most beautiful in the Chihuahuan sierras. Few Anglo-Americans have ever reached Tomochic; until the mid-1960s the only access to the village was by foot or pack train. No wheeled vehicle ever entered the little valley unless it had been disassembled first and carried on burros or mules. The difficulty lay in the fact that the Valley of Tomochic is shaped like a sweet potato. Starting at the south where the Río Tomochic comes through a narrow gorge in the mountains, the valley broadens to about a mile in width and extends a distance of three miles, ending on the north where the river exits through another narrow pass.

To understand the impact of Teresita upon Tomochic, and

the tragedy that resulted, it is important to know something of the people and their heritage. The first contact of the Indians of Tomochic with Europeans occurred in the early 1600s when mines yielding gold, copper and silver were opened in the adjacent region. Although the engineers, foremen and overseers were all Spaniards, the mine laborers were conscripted Tarahumara men. Other Spanish groups included the conductors of mule and burro caravans, constantly in transit back and forth, bringing in supplies and carting away the crude bars of precious metals. For the conductors and their crew, the Valley of Tomochic offered a convenient and delightful place to camp.

In 1653 the Tarahumaras rebelled against conscription by the mining companies. Armed with knives, bows and arrows, the laborers gave vent to their fierce resentment of slave status. The viceroy sent an army with European weapons to subdue the insurrection and restore the status quo. The Spaniards and mestizos who made up the army camped in Tomochic for four years.

The Spanish miners, convoy conductors, guards and soldiers were lusty and ruthless men. Deprived of women of their own race and station, they freely satisfied their urges with Tarahumara women. As a result there appeared in Tomochic, as in similar localities throughout Mexico, a race of half-breed children who were raised as Indians by their native mothers. When the next generation of Spanish miners and mule drivers arrived, they found a crop of mestiza maidens to choose from. Because the mestizas more closely resembled the women of their own race, the Spaniards favored them, and many actually married their half-breed sweethearts. When a mestiza married a Spaniard, she made the transition from an Indian way of life to the social and economic status of mestizos. The offspring in turn were three-quarter Caucasian, a ratio of Indian and Spanish blood prevalent in Tomochic until the 1800s. Over a period of a century, therefore, the village was transformed from an Indian settlement into a mestizo, or "white," pueblo. The pure Tarahumaras moved away to other places where they maintained their tribal integrity.

Out of the racial mixture in Tomochic a rather singular physical type emerged. From their Tarahumara great-grandmothers, the men inherited enormous barrel chests and huge lungs, useful in high altitudes. The inheritance also included remarkable stamina. By their Spanish ancestors, whose characteristics predominated, they were endowed with tall and powerful physiques, light complexions, brown eyes and heavy black beards. Somewhere in the mixture they inherited resided a stubborn and proudly independent spirit.

For over a century, the Tomochitecos defended their village against the ever-present menace of Apache raids. The men lived with their guns—more recently, American-made repeating Winchesters. Even when working in the fields they carried rifles strapped to their backs. They abstained from strong drink, their nerves were steady and their aim deadly; when provoked, the Tomochitecos displayed courageous defiance. Side by side with these traits, another characteristic of these people developed. They were devoutly, even fanatically, religious.

The religious zeal of the Tomochitecos was fostered in part by an extraordinary priest who arrived almost half a century after the first Jesuit missionaries built a church in the area in 1676. In 1722 Father Jorge Hostranck, an astute German member of the Jesuit order, took over the mission, and for forty-one years exerted a profound influence on the inhabitants. In addition to teaching his parishioners the tenets of the Church and the human virtues of personal integrity and dignity, he instructed them in agriculture, animal husbandry, weaving and other manual skills. Father Hostranck left an indelible imprint on the Tomochiteco character. Four years after the beloved padre died, the Jesuit order was expelled from Mexico. Yet so devout were the Tomochitecos that on their own, under lay leaders, they continued the religious organization and activities of their revered Father Jorge.

After a time the Franciscans came to take over where the Jesuits had left off, building a small mission adjacent to the church in Tomochic. Here religious instruction was emphasized, and the people of the village flocked to the new priests for learning. With the War of Independence and the establishment of the state of Sonora in 1825, the Franciscans withdrew, leaving Tomochic to the secular arm of the Church. No regular priest was ever stationed there again, although at long intervals one would pass through, hold Mass, and perform weddings and baptisms. Nonetheless, the people continued to observe their faith under secular leaders, and lay priests with great power and conviction fired them with zeal for religious activities. With little education and scant regard for Catholic tradition, the Tomochitecos eventually developed a schismatic theology of their own.

In 1890 the leader of the lay priests at Tomochic was Cruz Chávez, a tall man of imposing build with typical Tomochiteco characteristics: wide torso, broad shoulders and a narrow waist. Framed by a heavy beard, his long face and large, dark brown eyes revealed an audacious and obstinate spirit. Every one of his actions and judgments was motivated by religious impulse. As persuasive an orator as William Jennings Bryan, Chávez displayed as well the zealotry of a John Brown, the simplicity of a Buddhist monk, and the militancy of a Joshua. He became the unquestioned leader of the people of Tomochic, with the exception of a few of the wealthy and pretentious families who owned the best fields and the most cattle and goats.

The Díaz government in Tomochic was represented by two other men with the name of Chávez—unrelated to Cruz but kin to each other. Juan Ignacio Chávez represented the political arm of the regime, and Captain Joaquin Chávez served the interests of the military, even though no soldiers were stationed at Tomochic. It was the captain's duty to watch for and gather evidence of treason. From time to time he also commanded the armed escorts for pack trains operating between the neighboring English-owned mines and Chihuahua City. Both Ignacio and Joaquin were heartily disliked by most of the people in the village.

In a sense, Cruz Chávez and his followers resembled Amish settlers in the United States in that they were a self-sufficient community of industrious and hard-working providers. The Tomo-chitecos diligently tilled their little fields. They raised and stored crops of corn, beans and pumpkins, killed their hogs and cured the meat, and tended their cattle and goats on the mountainsides. They butchered beeves for fresh meat and for making jerky. Their excellent marksmanship also served them well in hunting, enabling families to supplement their diet with wild game such as deer, bear and turkey. Any free time left over after their labors the Tomochitecos devoted to religious worship, along with all the attendant rituals surrounding omens, prophecies and supernatural phenomena. By virtue of this preoccupation their daily lives were as restrictive as those of the early Pilgrims of New England.

When reports of Teresita's "miracles" came to Tomochic, Cruz organized an expedition comprising a dozen men to go with him to Cabora and investigate the truth of the reports. The group cunningly included a suitable test invalid, José Ramírez, an old man from a nearby village encumbered with a tumor the size of a turkey egg at the base of his skull. The Tomochitecos arrived at Cabora with hundreds of other pilgrims, all displaying the same reverent and humble attitudes before Teresita. Unlike the other visitors, however, the followers of Cruz Chávez were easily distinguished by their heavy beards and tall, proud bearing. The fact that each man had a repeating Winchester of recent make slung across his back also served to set the group apart, especially in the eyes of the government spies.

The Tomochitecos studied the ministrations of Teresita for several days, witnessing cures that seemed truly miraculous. They noted the gentleness and compassion she accorded the incurables, and how they departed reconciled to their fate. Each day their enthusiasm and belief in her abilities increased. Eager to make the acquaintance of this saintly young woman, Chávez arranged an audience with her secretary, Amado Corral. The meeting took place that evening in Teresita's house. Although apparently this was the only time Chávez talked with her, he evidently made a considerable impression, because during the next two years, through her secretary, Teresita carried on an extensive correspondence with the Tomochiteco leader.

The day after the meeting, José Ramírez asked Teresita to cure the tumor on his neck. When she had completed her treatment, she took note of the old man's kindly, wrinkled face, framed by a snowy mane of hair and beard. In a pleasant, joking voice, she said, "You have the appearance of San José."

The old man, flattered and somewhat bewildered, knelt and gazed up at her in great humility. He kissed her hand, muttering "Blessed Teresa."

The tumor eventually disappeared, but all José could later remember of that fateful day were Teresita's words comparing him to St. Joseph. He solemnly told his companions that Teresita had called him a "saint," meaning she had "conferred sainthood" on him. So strong was the faith of Chávez and his men that they willingly accepted this sudden, beatific promotion. "San José" decided that since he was a saint he must act like one. Saints, he decided, did not possess worldly goods, women or dependents. Immediately upon his return, he sent his second wife, as well as a daughter by his first wife, to his drunkard half-brother Bernardo in Guerrero. Then he divested himself of his little house and all else he owned, depending entirely upon the village to see that he received sustenance fit for a saint. This self-inflicted chastity and poverty, preceded by the awesome cure of the tumor, greatly impressed the people of Tomochic.

After the group's return, Cruz Chávez called a meeting at the church and fascinated his audience with glowing accounts of the miraculous powers of Saint Teresa of Cabora. Then and there, the people of Tomochic, acting as a congregation, voted to throw out their dead saints and adopt live ones. The Saint of Cabora became the official guardian of Tomochic, with "San José" elected a sort of honorary saint, relegated to second place because he had not performed any miracles. The wooden statue of the previous village saint was removed from its niche in the church, and a statue of Santa Teresa, freshly carved and painted, was placed in its stead.

With the installation of the statue, the Tomochitecos waxed even more dedicated and impassioned than before, spending hours in church each day, devoutly absorbed in prayer and contemplation. As the schismatic practices of worship increased, the conventional liturgy of the Church was replaced by new forms, all of them the inventions of Cruz Chávez. He composed his own prayers and delivered them in a powerful and persuasive voice. These stirring and exhilarating exhortations kept the emotions of his people roused to intense fervor.

Underlying their leader's own heightened dedication was his new-found adoration of the Saint of Cabora. From his conversations with her, Chávez had distilled the essence of her creed: the power of God, love and good works, tempered by justice.

Concentrating upon their devotions, the leaders failed to observe that a potentially explosive situation was in the making at Tomochic. Some fifteen young men in their late teens had begun the practice of leaving home at intervals to work in the neighboring mines. Although the wages were low, they could make more in the mines than they could by herding cattle or goats for the wealthy Domínguez or Ledesma families at home or by serving as guards in Captain Joaquin Chávez's convoy. After working for several weeks, the young workers would return to the village with a few pesos. At home they would shoot some firecrackers, dance and "make a fiesta" until their money was squandered, at which point the boys returned to the mines again. Their refusal to work for the local families or to serve in the convoys infuriated Captain Chávez. He threatened to conscript them all and send them to the army.

At that time, conscription was the most dreaded of punishments for mestizos. It was similar to being condemned for the better part of one's life to the penitentiary and spending it on a chain gang. If a conscript managed to escape, he was sure to be picked up somewhere, sometime, and summarily shot. If he did not attempt escape but tried to serve his period, he lived at the caprice of the officers. Under the terms of the *Ley Fuga*, an officer could shoot a soldier with little or no provocation and never be required to answer for the crime. When Captain Chávez threatened to hand the young men over to the army, bitter resentment flared in Tomochic.

Another government threat constantly looming was the possibility that the *Ley Lerdo* might be invoked against the village. In dealing with the Indians, the government took their lands with no hesitation or recompense and awarded them to *hacendados*. In the case of mestizo villages, some legal niceties were observed as a concession to the inhabitants. The government's usual technique was to divide the village public lands among the heads of families, giving each family title to a particular plot. The plots might be badly situated, devoid of water or covered by poor soil, for the government never intended the mestizos to eke a living from their barren little patches of land. An agent of some *hacendado* with designs on the village soon appeared with an offer to purchase the holdings. Because the plots were of little value, or because the prospect of a few pesos in hand was overpowering, one by one the villagers usually agreed to sell. In a few years the *hacendado* became the legal owner of the village and its lands, and the once-independent mestizos were his peons.

Some of the more intelligent and farsighted men of Tomochic, like Cruz Chávez, knew that this fate could befall Tomochic. At any moment a mining company might decide that there were minerals under village lands, or a lumber company might look covetously at its virgin forests. Apprehensive and suspicious, the leaders of Tomochic grew more and more hostile toward the central government.

In December 1891 a string of related incidents occurred that eventually led to rebellion in the village. Unknown to the Tomochitecos, the spread of a Teresita cult throughout the sierras had caused considerable alarm among priests, who feared the growth of a heretical, schismatic movement in Mexico. To them, she was no longer a simple faith healer but rather an insidious threat to the Church. And they denounced her from their pulpits as a heretic.

Most vehement among the anti-Teresita priests was Father Manuel Gustelúm of Uranchic. Leaving Cabora after the failure of his "hat-pin" scheme, he became even more belligerent, and traveled from village to village preaching against Teresa Urrea. In December he arrived at Tomochic and instructed the sacristan of the church to assemble the congregation for Mass, telling the man that he intended to deliver a sermon against heresy in the village. The sacristan, a loyal Tomochiteco, relayed the purpose of the priest's visit at the same time that he spread news of the Mass.

Before the service, however, Cruz Chávez called his followers to a meeting at his house. Included were all the inhabitants of the village except the two Díaz-appointed Chávez families and the wealthy Domínguez and López families. Alarmed by the potential threat of Father Gustelúm's Mass, the congregation exchanged various ideas regarding how the worshippers should react. It was decided that the villagers would attend and listen to what he had to say, and that Cruz alone would respond, giving the position of the Tomochitecos.

Gustelúm warmed to his subject with caustic and fiery vigor. Teresita was a monstrosity from hell, Satan incarnate. Her ministrations were diabolical; her cures the work of the devil. The people of Tomochic were idiotic dupes. If they did not come to their senses at once, denounce La Niña de Cabora, and desist from this heresy, they would all be excommunicated forever.

The congregation listened until the priest had finished his diatribe. Then Cruz Chávez took the pulpit. In contrast to the impassioned denouncements of the priest, he calmly and quietly explained why the Tomochitecos believed in the Saint of Cabora. Many of them had seen her, she was pure and good, her teachings were the same as those of Christ, and her good works conformed to those advocated by Christ. In short, he concluded, the people of Tomochic had no intention of denouncing her.

By the time Chávez had finished, Father Gustelúm was so incensed that he could hardly contain himself. Livid with rage, the veins in his temples and neck swollen and throbbing, he stamped to the pulpit to deliver a rebuttal. At the signal of Chávez, the congregation silently rose and filed out of the church, leaving the outraged priest glowering at their backs in helpless fury.

Stalking out of the church, Father Gustelúm quickly departed for Uranchic. Upon reaching his village, Gustelúm immediately dispatched a runner to Chihuahua City with a message to the governor stating that the people of Tomochic were in a state of revolt.

As luck would have it, the Tomochitecos had already made the acquaintance of the governor of Chihuahua under circumstances by no means favorable to their cause. The year before, Governor Lauro Carillo had completed a tour of the sierran villages. At Tomochic he was treated with respect and courtesy. While visiting the church he noticed two paintings of artistic merit. One was of San Joaquín and the other of Santa Ana. Both were purported to have been painted by the famous Spanish artist Bartoloméo Murillo. They may have been copies, for at that time many great religious paintings were reproduced by competent artists in Mexico. Whether original or copies, Carillo was quite taken by the works. His term of office was due to expire in 1892 and he was anxious to be "re-elected." This could be done easily if President Díaz sent the proper instructions to his henchmen in Chihuahua. It occurred to Carillo that a valuable present to the dictator's wife, Carmen, might enhance his chances of another term. He remembered the paintings at Tomochic and sent instructions to the political chief of the district, a man named Silviano Gonzales, to proceed to the village, obtain the paintings by any means, and send them back to the governor.

Gonzales picked up two cheap pictures at random, went to Tomochic, and told the sacristan that he had come to exchange some new pictures for the old ones. The sacristan was suspicious of the proposal and slipped away to inform Cruz Chávez. As soon as he was gone, Gonzales quickly cut the old paintings from their frames and inserted the cheap canvases in their stead. He rolled the originals under his arm and hastily made ready to leave.

Outside the church, however, he was confronted by some thirty armed Tomochitecos. Chávez ordered him to return the paintings to their places in the church. Gonzales explained that he had taken the works by the order of Governor Carillo, who wanted to send them as a present to Carmelita, the wife of the president. This argument made little impression on the men of Tomochic. Chávez answered that if the governor wished to curry favor with Díaz he should in truth purchase his gifts, not steal them from the poor people of a mountain village. It was the duty of the governor, moreover, to set a good example for honesty and integrity. Gonzales reluctantly and sullenly returned the paintings to the church. But no sooner had he arrived in Guerrero than he sent a message to Governor Carillo accusing the people of Tomochic of being dangerous rebels.

Before long, a third event further fueled this highly inflammable situation. Captain Joaquín Chávez, on his way from the Palos Altos mine with a convoy carrying silver bars, maliciously informed the English manager of the mine that he would have to make a long detour around Tomochic because he feared the young men there would attempt a holdup of the caravan. After the departure of the convoy, the exasperated manager sent a telegram to the central government in Mexico City, complaining of the "lawless" state of affairs in Tomochic and requesting that steps be taken to protect the company's property.

Word of the telegram was brought to Tomochic. Cruz Chávez immediately sent a message to the manager of the mine declaring the report unjust. Never in two hundred years, he asserted, had the Tomochitecos molested a passing pack train. Indeed, if the manager was uneasy, the Tomochitecos themselves would conduct the caravan as far as Guerrero. The manager did not bother to retract his message to Mexico City and President Díaz telegraphed Governor Carillo to investigate the disturbances at Tomochic.

Thus it happened that the distorted complaints of Father Gustelúm, the inflammatory report of the district political chief Gonzales, and the unjustified grievance of the manager of the English mine all arrived on the governor's desk in Chihuahua City within a short time of one another.

A series of tragic events was set in motion when, on November 25, 1891, forces from a battalion of the federal army and auxiliary soldiers under Captain Joaquín Chávez were ordered to Tomochic to put down the "rebellion." The villagers were praying in the church when someone rushed in and reported that the town was surrounded by federal troops. The Tomochitecos poured out of the building and saw the government forces attacking without explanation or warning. Always armed, the villagers fought a retiring skirmish to their homes. One Tomochiteco was killed and several wounded. Cruz Chávez and twenty-eight of his men, not wishing to oppose the federal forces, withdrew from Tomochic to the village of Tutuaca, about fifteen miles to the northwest, and set up a small camp.

The troops took over the town and searched the houses—fruitlessly in most cases—for arms, killing or wounding several Tomochitecos in the process. They also appropriated much of the food the people had stored for winter. After a few days, troops from another battalion, the Eleventh, under Captain Francisco Castro, were ordered to Palos Altos, presumably to guard the English mine. Captain Joaquín Chávez, accompanied by some Tomochiteco prisoners, returned to Guerrero to report that the "rebellion" at Tomochic had been quelled.

Cruz Chávez and his men remained several days at Tutuaca while debating a plan of action. They realized that they were now

J. CISNEROS

classed as rebels by the government, though the reasons remained a mystery. No explanation had been given them. To return to their village and hand themselves over to the federal authorities would mean conscription. They would be scattered in distant garrisons of the country, and none, probably, would ever see his family again. In desperation the little band decided to go as a group to Cabora and seek the counsel of La Santa. Leaving Tutuaca, they set out on the road that led past Yecora, Nuri and Baroyeca. Because the government had informants everywhere, the destination of the Tomochitecos was quickly discovered and the information sent to Guerrero by messenger. The news was relayed by telegraph to Chihuahua City and thence to Mexico City.

President Díaz immediately wired General José T. Otero, commander of the Mayo Zone at Huatabampo, Sonora, directing him to dispatch a force to apprehend Chávez and his men at the ranch of Cabora. He also ordered Teresa Urrea placed under surveillance and alerted the federal army headquarters at the Yaqui Zone at Torim. At the same time, Governor Carillo ordered Commandante Ramón G. Ochoa to follow the Tomochitecos' trail with eighty men and overtake them before they reached Cabora.

Chapter Thirteen

EARLY IN THE MORNING of Christmas Eve 1891, Teresita knelt in her chapel as usual, in silent devotion before a simple altar. Originally a bedroom in the south wing of the Casa Grande, the chamber had been converted into a chapel at Teresita's request. A doorway was opened in the west side of the room, facing Teresita's house, so that she could come directly across to the chapel without having to make a detour through the compound. The room thus had two doors: the original entrance opening onto the veranda, and the new entry. Furnishings in the chapel were sparse and simple, stripped of holy images or pictures of saints. By this time Teresita's religious concepts had developed past the point of considering necessary the adoration of saints or the intercession of priests.

Suddenly the door to the veranda opened and Don Tomás abruptly entered. "I'm sorry to interrupt you, my child. A company of federal cavalry is approaching from the south, and I want your promise to stay in this room until we learn why troops should be coming at this hour." His voice betrayed his anxiety.

Teresita, still kneeling before the candlelit altar, nodded compliance and remained where she was. Don Tomás crossed to the west door, locked it, went back out the exit to the veranda, locked it as well from the outside, and put the keys in his pocket.

By this time his four Urrea sons, who were then at Cabora, had gathered in the compound and were watching the cavalry troops, now halted near the big corral to the south. Eyeing the troops, Don Tomás spoke incisively to the boys, as if giving military orders.

"I fear they have come to take Teresita. We will not permit it. Get your rifles."

The boys, sharing their father's defiance, immediately ran for their guns. Don Tomás hastened to his room and presently returned with both pistols strapped to his waist. By this time an officer was approaching from the corral on foot. Don Tomás stationed each of his sons behind the pillars of the veranda near the chapel door. He himself waited in the compound in front of the door. As the officer drew near, Don Tomás recognized him as Captain Emilio Enríquez, a man with whom he had been on friendly terms for years. The captain seemed embarrassed.

"Good day, Don Tomás. I apologize for this intrusion and for coming at this hour, but I am here under orders of General Bandala at Huatabampo. We have information from Mexico City that a party of armed rebels from Tomochic is coming here to confer with your daughter Teresa. We are here to apprehend them."

Don Tomás disguised his instant awareness that this was the danger he had long feared. "I cannot believe that the Tomochitecos have risen in rebellion against the government," he responded. "These men were here at the ranch last year. They came peacefully and behaved like all the other pilgrims."

"We've been informed that they made a proclamation: they will respect no authority but that of God. They have elected your daughter Teresa as their "saint." As such she is expected to interpret God's will to them, and this is why they are coming here to see her. The authorities in Chihuahua believe your daughter has incited them to revolt."

"Impossible!" Don Tomás retorted hotly. "Teresita never discussed politics with anyone!"

"Perhaps you are right, Don Tomás, but the government is convinced she is using her curing powers to teach sedition. I regret to inform you that I have orders to place her under arrest."

Don Tomás's eyes grew cold; his voice became sharp and menacing. "Captain Enríquez, my daughter is in that room. The door is locked, and I have the key. Before you arrest her, you will have to kill me and my four sons." He motioned toward the veranda and the four boys tensely holding their Winchesters.

Captain Enríquez hesitated as he appraised the situation. Then he turned to Don Tomás. "I understand your position. I will withdraw my troops along the road for a mile. There we will confer and let you know our decision."

As he walked briskly away, Don Tomás motioned to his sons. "Quick! Saddle two horses. The captain is giving us a chance to get Teresita away."

"Yes, but where will you go?" asked Buenaventura.

"To the sierras," Antonio suggested.

"To the Bacatete Mountains with the Yaquis," offered Miguel.

Don Tomás shook his head. "No, that would be an admission of guilt. We must go to the government authorities and ask protection. We have done nothing to cause trouble. I will take Teresita to Cocorit and place ourselves in the custody of General Torres. True, he is our enemy, but he is not as tricky as General Bandala."

"Then we will go with you," said Antonio.

"No. You must all stay here to look after the ranch and the people. Antonio, you will be in charge."

Within minutes, Don Tomás and Teresita set off on horseback in the direction away from Captain Enríquez's troops. The horses galloped along the road to the northwest, toward Cocorit.

At the ranch, meanwhile, the crowds of visitors milled about anxiously, confused by the presence of federal troops and La Santa's sudden departure. During the day the troops leaked word that a rebel army (its size greatly exaggerated) was coming from the sierras of Chihuahua. Many pilgrims hastily left the area, but others stayed to see what would happen.

When Captain Enríquez returned to the chapel, Antonio met him in the compound.

"What is the decision of Don Tomás?" asked the captain, showing no surprise that the *patrón* himself was not present.

"My father and Teresita are on their way to Cocorit to present themselves to the authorities there."

"Good. I am relieved of that responsibility. Now I have but one other disagreeable task. I am ordered to search these premises for arms and munitions."

For a moment Antonio demurred, then agreed to the search. "Very well. My brothers and I will assist you. We have nothing to hide."

The entire day before Christmas was given over to a thorough search of the ranch buildings. The Casa Grande, Teresita's house, the homes of the *mayordomos*, and all the ramadas of the vaqueros and field workers were inspected. Nothing was found other than the arms necessary for the operation of the ranch. Captain Enríquez, who was courteous and considerate throughout the search, refused to take arms from the people of the ranch. The weapons were not concealed, and there was no evidence that they were intended for seditious activities. That night his troops camped outside the compound of the Casa Grande, sentries were posted, and precautions were taken against a surprise attack by the Tomochitecos.

On Christmas day Enríquez decided to go forward and meet the "rebels." In the afternoon he set out with his troops on the road to Baroyeca, a route he was reasonably sure the Tomochitecos would be following. He camped that evening at Las Vacas ranch. On the next morning, the 26th, he resumed his march. Within an hour the troops reached a narrow valley called El Alamo de los Palomares, so named because of a cottonwood tree that stood on a ranch once owned by the Palomares family.

Here Cruz Chávez and his twenty-seven Tomochitecos were

waiting, concealed by trees and shrubbery. Shouting "Viva la Santa de Cabora," the Tomochitecos fired the first volley. Desultory firing came from the troops. A second volley from Chávez and his men caused the federal soldiers to panic, and they rode back in wild disorder, scattering, and leaving Captain Enríquez, his first lieutenant and six troopers dead, and several wounded. The battle was over within minutes. Only one of the Tomochitecos, José Chávez, younger brother of Cruz, was wounded.

Cruz went through the pockets and effects of the dead officers. On the body of Enríquez they found official papers. Reading these, he learned the purpose of the mission against him. He also discovered that Commander Ochoa was following the Tomochitecos and that Teresa Urrea wa ssuspected of having caused the "rebellion" at Tomochic and was to be put under surveillance. Leaving the dead and wounded federal troops, Cruz and his men pushed rapidly on to Cabora.

The tall, powerful Tomochitecos, with their fierce eyes and tattered clothes, created great excitement as they marched up to the ranch. The Urrea sons met Cruz and his men in the compound.

"We are here to see the Saint of Cabora," Cruz announced.

"She and my father have gone to Cocorit to give themselves over to the authorities," Antonio replied.

Cruz could hardly believe what he heard. "Why should they do that?"

"To avoid being arrested by General Otero, who has a personal grudge against my father."

Cruz and his men could not hide their disappointment. Tears came to the eyes of these rugged mountain men when they learned that Teresita had gone away.

Affected by their emotions, Antonio waited an interval before adding, "The government believes that our sister has taught sedition to the people of the sierras. Your coming here helps to substantiate those charges. She and our father are in grave danger. If you are truly devoted to her, do not attempt to see her. Leave here at once. Go back to your homes."

Cruz Chávez would not give up so easily. "How many troops are stationed at Cocorit?" he asked.

"Many. Several hundred."

Cruz considered the odds against vanquishing such a large force. "Very well. We will go back to our village, but first we would ask a favor."

"Yes?"

"We would like to worship in the chapel of Santa Teresa."

"Very well. But make haste. Colonel Torres and his troops may arrive at any time."

Antonio opened the veranda door to the chapel with the keys his father had left him. Chávez leaned his rifle against the wall of the veranda, removed his hat and entered. Each of the Tomochitecos followed suit. Inside, they knelt, Cruz directly in front of the altar. After he had delivered a prayer of his own composing, he stood and exhorted his men on the virtues of La Santa. Then he led the group in a rousing hymn. For two hours, the prayers, songs and exhortations continued as the emotions in the chapel reached a fevered pitch. Several men began to weep unashamedly. It was a fervent farewell: the men on their knees on the cold stone, their faces lifted to the light of the flames burning on the altar of their living saint, and their leader before them, casting a giant shadow on the wall behind the altar.

Antonio and his brothers waited uneasily, listening to the resounding service from the veranda steps. At length the bearded men emerged from the chapel, gathered their rifles, and shook hands sadly with the Urrea sons. They set off along the road they had come, leaving behind the wounded José Chávez, who was convinced that Teresita would soon return to heal him.

Teresita and her father arrived at Cocorit on Christmas Eve. Colonel Lorenzo Torres, commandant of the garrison, received them with pompous and disdainful insolence. For three days he kept them under house arrest, all the while busily sending telegrams to Guaymas, Huatabampo and Mexico City. On the 27th he received news of the defeat of Captain Enríquez and was commanded to take two hundred troops and pursue the rebels with all speed. Don Tomás and Teresita were ordered to accompany the regiment to Cabora.

At Cabora the colonel informed them that they were free for the time being; General Otero's orders had been to keep them under surveillance, not under arrest. Don Tomás learned from his sons of the wounded Tomochiteco, José Chávez, and turned the man over to the colonel, making it clear that he expected the prisoner to be treated humanely.

Torres wasted little time at the ranch. With José Chávez in tow, he followed the trail of the Tomochitecos and reached the battleground at the Alamo de los Palomares. The bloated bodies of the Enríquez troops, still unburied, lay scattered where they had fallen. In a fit of outrage and vengeance, Torres stood José beside the road and shot him to death.

Torres then pressed on to Santa Ana, where he met up with Commander Ochoa. Somehow Chávez and his men had managed to slip by Ochoa undetected. Ochoa joined forces with Torres; their combined strength now numbered some three hundred against twenty-seven Tomochitecos. Several times they came close enough to the wily mountain men to engage in running skirmishes. Successfully dodging the enemy bullets, the Tomochitecos killed and wounded several government troops. More than once the Chávez group could have inflicted great damage, but Cruz seemed anxious to avoid further conflicts. On December 31st, at the Chihuahuan border, Torres gave up the chase and returned to his base. Ochoa, too, lost all desire for tangling with the Tomochitecos and ordered his men back to Palos Altos, where they disbanded.

Cruz Chávez and his men returned to Tomochic on February 2, 1892. By direct march the band could have reached home in two days; how and where they passed the other thirty-one days is not on record. However, when they did return they displayed a considerable number of new, repeater Winchester rifles and a sizable supply of ammunition. The most likely source for such contraband was the Arizona Territory.

Chapter Fourteen

AFTER THE SPREAD OF Teresita's fame in 1890, a wave of religious fanaticism, as fervent as that in the mestizo villages of the Sierra Madres, swept through the Indian settlements along the Río Mayo.

Each village had its own political leaders, called *jefes* (governors), as well as lay priests and witches. The villagers worshipped a variety of saints, some of whom were canonized by the Roman Church, others of whom were still living and did not belong to the official Catholic hierarchy.

In a few of the Mayo villages, any inhabitant whose behavior did not conform to that of other villagers might have local sainthood bestowed on him or her. In one village the living saint was Santa Domian, a sixteen-year-old girl; other live village saints included Santa Camila, Santa Isabel, Santa Juana, San Ireneo and San Luís. After 1890 these native "holy" figures were superseded by one whose powers were truly awe-inspiring, "La Niña de Cabora." Individually and in groups, the Mayos made repeated pilgrimages to Cabora to observe and adore Teresita, from the latter part of 1890 to the first half of 1892.

On May 15, 1892, a group of about two hundred Mayo Indians, led by Juan Tebas and Miguel Terigoqui, attacked the town of Navojoa, shouting "Viva la Santa de Cabora!" They were repulsed by the federal garrison assisted by armed citizens. Several local citizens were killed, including the municipal president. The Mayo casualties included eleven dead in the battle and twenty-seven more hunted down and killed. Others who participated in the attack on Navojoa scattered and hid out in the desert jungle of mesquite, cholla and sahuaro—cover so dense that in places a man more than a yard away could not be seen.

This was a season sacred to the Mayos. Their religion, like that of the Yaquis, was a mixture of Roman Catholicism and pre-Columbian paganism, ritually celebrated with the aid of witch doctors, magic, hexes, saints and priests. The Mayo villages, each of which represented a religious unit, were scattered along the Río Mayo at intervals of four to six miles. Family ramadas were not concentrated around the large structure that served as a church, but were scattered in the jungle along the river, never more than a mile away because the river was their only source of water. Also situated along the river at distances of ten to twelve miles were federal garrisons with squadrons reporting to head-quarters at Huatabampo.

It was later ascertained that the Mayos who attacked Navojoa, a mestizo town whose merchants had exploited the Indians, were a local group filled with a deep resentment against the Díaz government for having appropriated their lands and given them to rich Mexicans and Americans. Carried away by religious zeal and believing that the beneficent Saint of Cabora would protect and shield them, they organized an impromptu attack on the town. It is not known if their courage and ill-advised decision were actually triggered by one too many rounds of *mezcal* or by an overdose of religious fervor.

When news of the attack on Navojoa reached Huatabampo, General Abraham Bandala assumed there was a general uprising among the Indians, and sent Captain Rivera with a squadron posthaste up the Mayo River, picking up other squadrons as he went. The lower Mayo villages knew nothing of the fighting at

Navojoa, but every group encountered was put under guard and sent back to Huatabampo. Because news of the advance of federal troops traveled faster than the troops themselves, some of the Indians, forewarned, had just enough time to start out for Cabora, where they believed the magical powers of Saint Teresa would protect them. Word that the Mayos were converging on Cabora, together with reports of the Indian battle cry at Navojoa, convinced General Bandala that the rebellion had been implemented and directed from Cabora. Supported by a hundred troops, the general started toward the ranch. At Guadalupe he met General Otero heading south from Cocorit. Joining forces, they turned east toward Cabora, fully expecting to meet with an overwhelming assemblage of Mayo warriors ready for battle. On arrival they were chagrined to find nothing out of the ordinary. In actuality the Mexican government had sent five hundred soldiers to confront one nineteen-year-old girl.

Although he had been warned in advance of General Bandala's approach, Don Tomás made no effort to prepare for an encounter or to flee with Teresita. Instead he waited with outward calmness for the arrival of the federal forces. Bandala informed Don Tomás that he had instructions from the secretary of war to arrest Teresita and dispatch her under military guard to Nogales, where she would be sent across the international border into the United States. The penalty for returning to Mexico would be a firing squad. Don Tomás quietly asked the reasons for her exile. The general replied that the government considered her a dangerous agitator and ascribed the rebellions at Tomochic to her influence. Don Tomás argued long and heatedly against the charges, but Bandala remained unmoved. She could go peacefully, he said, or they would take her by force. When Don Tomás was convinced at last that there was no alternative, he declared calmly, "Then if she goes, I go with her."

"But we have no instructions to take you," the general replied. "You are not included in the orders."

"If you take her without me, it will be over my dead body."

"Very well. My orders do not state that you shall not go. So you may go, but only you. No family. No servants."

"But I need time to arrange my affairs."

"You have only until tomorrow morning. We will bivouac here tonight. You will forgive us if we mount a heavy guard around your house until we leave."

"How will Teresita and I travel?"

"Any way you wish. Horseback, carriage, wagon."

"And what route shall we travel?"

"That is for me alone to determine. Not even my officers will know until an hour ahead of time when we will leave or what direction we will take."

Teresita's reaction to Bandala's orders has not been revealed either by the military records or by any accounts handed down by the family. Undoubtedly it was a night of shock, confusion, hasty decisions, preparations and tremendous sorrow. Gabriela was pregnant with her fifth child, and her other children ranged in age from two to seven years. Don Tomás assured her that he would send for her and the children as soon as arrangements could be made. He sent for his *mayordomos* and conferred for hours with them and his older boys on the management of the farms and cattle. In addition to keeping up the household at Cabora, the farms and ranches would have to continue to support Doña Loreto and his daughters in Alamos as well as the two exiles in the United States. Don Tomás discussed tentative plans for bringing Gabriela, her children and Teresita's staff as soon as he and Teresita were settled. Teresita herself spent most of the night consoling Mariana and Josefina, while the three of them decided what she could take in one small chest.

Next morning the column was formed. The rear seat of a carriage was loaded with two chests, one for Teresita and another belonging to Don Tomás, both with bedrolls tied behind. Teresita rode in the front seat beside an army driver. Don Tomás was invited to ride at the head of the column with General Otero. Officiously taking charge, General Bandala chose to ride up and

down the column to oversee all aspects of the march. At noon the column paused at Guadalupe to water the horses and feed the troops, and then continued north toward Cajame and Cocorit.

About mid-afternoon General Bandala pulled his mount up beside Teresita's carriage and ordered the driver to stop. He dismounted, threw his horse's reins to the driver, and told him to mount his horse and follow; the general himself would drive the carriage. Now seated beside Teresita, Bandala apologized for the distasteful nature of his mission. Praising her devotion to the people and her good works, the general expressed a desire to be of help and offered to intercede with the president on her behalf. Then, much to the astonishment of his young prisoner, he asked Teresita to marry him. To this she responded with an unqualified rejection. Undaunted, the general came more to the point. At Cocorit he would provide her with a house where he would expect to rendezvous with her that night.

Teresita leaped from the carriage and turned to face her captor, who abruptly pulled the team up short. Standing beside the road, she threw her rebozo back over her shoulders. "Order me shot, General, but do not insult me!" she said in a low, fierce voice.

The general wordlessly climbed down from the carriage, motioned for his horse, and rode to the head of the column. That night the column bivouaced beside the road, and Teresita laid her bedroll next to that of Don Tomás for safety. The next morning she spoke to him in private.

"Papá, today I want you to ride with me or right behind the carriage."

"Why? Has someone bothered you?"

"Yes."

"Who?"

"General Bandala."

Don Tomás clenched his fists, his face reddened and his voice grew low and hard. "That bastard! Did he harm you?"

"No! No! Do nothing except stay near me."

Don Tomás half promised. But as soon as Teresita was safely on the carriage again, this time with a new driver, he slipped away and sought out General Bandala, indicating that he wanted to speak to him privately. When out of earshot of the troops, Don Tomás turned on him hotly.

"General Bandala, as an officer in the army I respect you, but as a man you do not come up to my ankle bone! If you ever molest my daughter again, either you or I will not get to our destination alive." He lifted his chin and stared straight at the officer.

The general visibly recoiled, and then turned and walked away. For the rest of the journey Don Tomás rode directly behind his daughter's carriage.

By the next day General Bandala had changed his previous plans for conducting the column personally all the way to Guaymas. Instead, he ordered a lieutenant with fifty dragoons to proceed with Don Tomás and Teresita to the port city. He warned the lieutenant to move with all speed where the road passed through Yaqui villages, ordering him to see that Teresita traveled with her face veiled so that she would not be recognized. If her presence should become known, reinforcements could be obtained at the military-zone headquarters at Torim. The main objective was to reach Guaymas without revealing to the Yaquis whom he was escorting.

The trip was made with no difficulties other than the humid 120-degree heat of early July. Some years later, in a newspaper interview, Teresita described her quarters in Guaymas: "I was put in prison, not in a jail but a guarded house where the mosquitoes ate on me all night." But the commandant of the Guaymas garrison had more than mosquitoes to worry about that night. No one could be sure that Teresita had not been recognized somewhere along the forty-mile stretch of road through Yaqui country. Yaquis had a way of seeing without being seen, and besides, some of them were psychic, or so he had heard.

The Sud Pacifico railway had only recently been completed

from Hermosillo, with train service established from Nogales three times a week each way. The trains usually consisted of two passenger coaches attached to a string of freight cars. The north-bound train was scheduled to leave the day after the escort arrived in Guaymas, and the commandant lost no time in arranging passage for "the most dangerous girl in Mexico." Empty boxcars were placed immediately before and behind one of the passenger coaches, with twenty-five soldiers alloted to each boxcar, some to ride inside and others on top, all fully armed.

As Teresita and her father approached the train, they were surrounded by swarms of soldiers, nervously alert to the first sounds of any Yaqui battle cry. The two prisoners were escorted into the passenger coach without incident. Looking out of the fly-stained windows, they saw a squad of soldiers approaching with a civilian in tow—another political prisoner, Don Tomás speculated. Suddenly Teresita recognized the man. "Look, Papá, it's Don Lauro Aguirre!" Don Tomás looked up, incredulous, as their old friend was escorted into the coach. Aguirre, too, it seemed, was high on the list of dangerous opponents to the Díaz regime. His presence made the thirty-hour trip to Nogales less wearisome, but the journey was not lacking in moments of tension and drama. The railroad from Guaymas traveled east, back toward Yaqui country, fifteen miles to Empalme. Here, where the switchyards and machine shop were located, the train stopped for some time while freight cars were switched in and out. To guard the halted coach, the soldiers from the boxcars fore and aft, assisted by troops from the local garrison, formed a shoulder-to-shoulder phalanx on either side of the passenger car containing the political prisoners.

From Empalme the railroad extended north for forty miles, running parallel to the Bacatete Mountains, a known stronghold of the Yaqui tribes. Along this stretch, the captain and lieutenant in charge of the escort rode inside the coach. Each kept a vigilant lookout through his field glasses, scanning the landscape on either side of the track. The other passengers became tense and silent as they watched the officers peer through the windows. On the top of the adjacent boxcars, soldiers crouched anxiously, rifles in hand. Only when the mountains were well behind them did the occupants of the coach relax and begin to talk to one another in normal voices.

Across the aisle from Teresita, a well-dressed woman tended her sick child, a baby girl who fretted and cried with every jolt of the train. As the day wore on, the child's condition grew worse until eventually a spasm wracked her small body. The child lay rigid, eyes rolling. Panicked, the mother cried for help. Teresita rose and steadied herself against the lurching of the coach. Taking the baby in her arms, she held it to her breast and whispered a few soft words while stroking the infant's quivering back. Almost immediately the spasm subsided, and the baby relaxed, looking up at the young woman with a happy smile. By this time all eyes were turned upon Teresita and the child. Teresita handed the child back to the mother and said, "Your baby is cured. She will be well now." Grateful and amazed, the woman stared at Teresita a few moments; then, grabbing her hand and kissing it, managed to blurt out, "You are the Blessed Teresa!"

Many of the other passengers stood to get a better look at the girl whose cures had made her famous throughout Mexico. By ones and twos they came toward her seat to speak to her. Several kissed her hand. She accepted their attention with modesty and dignity. The atmosphere in the coach was completely changed for the remainder of the journey. Even the captain was impressed by Teresita's composure and the awe she inspired in her admirers. At Nogales, he ordered a squad of soldiers to carry the baggage, and personally escorted the three political prisoners to the port of entry to the United States.

At that time only a barbed wire fence separated Nogales, Sonora, from Nogales, Territory of Arizona. The Mexican port officials had already been alerted to the arrival of the three political offenders, and they in turn had contacted United States officials. The chief of customs was waiting to welcome the refugees, fully aware that this was no ordinary occasion. Quickly clearing them, he wished them well in their new home. Before entering the hack that was to take them to a hotel, the three stood looking back through the gate at Mexico. Don Lauro could not resist a parting thrust. "I wonder," he said, "what will happen to a government that expels its nation's most gifted and Christlike woman."

On July 5, 1892, the Mexican consul in Nogales, Territory of Arizona, sent the secretary of war in Mexico City the following telegram:

"Teresa Urrea and father arrived here today."

Teresita's presence quickened the tempo of life in American Nogales as nothing ever had before in that small, notorious border town. News of her arrival spread rapidly in all directions. Mexicans and Indians from both sides of the border flocked into town, filling the streets and crowding the stores. Businessmen moved quickly to keep the girl a resident of their city, taking up a collection to purchase a house and lot. Because Teresita was not of legal age, they deeded the property to Don Tomás, who agreed to accept it as long as no favors were expected in return. As soon as a small staff of local assistants could be assembled, Teresita began seeing close to one hundred patients a day. With no experienced helpers, she sorely missed Mariana, Josefina and the other aides she had relied on at Cabora.

Lauro Aguirre urged her to ask nominal fees for her treatments, pointing out that in the United States people were accustomed to paying for medical services. Now that she had made the transfer from one country to another, it was a good time to plan her future on a realistic basis.

"No, Don Lauro. I can never charge for the use of the special powers God gave me. The Blessed Virgin said that I should help my fellow man. If I asked money, I would be using the powers for my own purposes."

Teresita remained adamant. Besides, as she pointed out to Don Lauro, the ranches in Sonora provided support for her father

148

and herself, and therefore she had no need of an income. No amount of attempted persuasion could change her mind, though Aguirre did not give up easily. Yet he had much else to keep him occupied in his new home.

Lauro Aguirre had been deported from Mexico because of his outspoken opposition to the policies of the Díaz government. At the time of his expulsion, his properties, which were considerable, had been confiscated. Once in the United States, he spoke out against the application of the *Ley Lerdo* to lands of the Indians and mestizos. He was against the economic aggrandizement of the few at the cost of peonage for the many, and he spoke with especial vehemence against the ruthlessness of the Díaz policies toward the Yaquis and Mayos, whom he had come to know well. Disgust with his native government turned him from a reformer into an active and dedicated revolutionist. Realizing that a revolution needs a philosophy and a mouthpiece, Aguirre established a newspaper, *El Progresista*, in Nogales, Arizona Territory, and dedicated it to the cause of freedom for the masses in Mexico.

Aguirre recognized the powerful asset Teresita's support could provide to the revolutionary movement. Her influence, already deep and broad among the people in three states—one-fourth of the Republic of Mexico—could be extended and developed through the power of the press. Although she had never counseled violence, her compassion for the plight of the Indians and poor mestizos was well known. If he could convert her spiritual influence into political rallying of these people, his chances of starting a true revolution would be greatly enhanced.

To Teresita and Don Tomás he confided his plan for overthrowing the dictator, and he urged Teresita to join him as associate editor of *El Progresista*. It was not necessary for her to work on the paper, he explained. She could continue to spend full time with her patients. The mere use of her name would attract people to the cause.

Teresita gravely shook her head. "No, Don Lauro, I cannot be a part of your plan. It would mean war and bloodshed. I believe change must come about peacefully, and that this can be brought about without the use of violence. Whatever influence I may have among these poor people is the result of love and good works. If I should now advocate hate and violence, my good works would be undone."

Aguirre did not press the matter further with Teresita. Shifting his ground, he insisted that Don Tomás join forces with him, sensing that the innately conservative nature of the *patrón* had been badly jarred by his expulsion. Again he received a firm, though gentle, refusal.

"No, Lauro, though I cannot tolerate Díaz and his lamentable actions, I cannot take a public stand against the dictator. As you know, my property has not yet been confiscated. My families are there now, and I am being closely watched by the Mexican consul here. If I make the slightest move in opposition to the government, Díaz will retaliate against my properties and my families."

Aguirre, although disappointed, decided to go it alone. Using every means at his command, he soon discovered support among the people of the area, and he became the nucleus for a group of Mexican malcontents, most of them of the firebrand variety. Indians and mestizos were now traveling back and forth across the border in large numbers to seek cures and consolation from Teresita. Aguirre's followers contacted and propagandized these Mexicans. The Mexican consul in Nogales grew worried and sent alarming reports to his superiors in Mexico City.

The Mexican government then decided it had acted unwisely in deporting the three and thereby losing control over their actions. An official request was made to United States authorities in Washington for the return of the Urreas and Aguirre to Mexico. Aguirre claimed, and was granted, the right of political asylum. Equally unwilling to fall into Díaz's hands again, Don Tomás rushed Teresita to Tucson and applied for American citizenship for them both. His application was accepted, but

Teresita was told that hers would have to be deferred for two years until she was of legal age.

This left Teresita still exposed to the danger of being kidnapped and taken back to Mexico. Soon after their return to Nogales, an attempt was made to seize her. No one, then or later, knew whether the effort was initiated by agents of the Mexican government or by agents of foreign investors, who knew they would lose their extensive holdings in the event of a revolution. Don Tomás was so disturbed by the attempted abduction that he decided to move Teresita away from the border, thus hoping to make kidnapping more difficult.

He found a ranch at a place called Bosque in the Santa Cruz Valley, about twenty miles north of Nogales and three miles from the old Spanish mission of Tumacorcori. Here, in addition to safety, he could enjoy horses, cows, chickens and more children around him. As soon as the household was settled, he sent to Cabora for Gabriela. He was anxious for her to come to Arizona so that her next child, due soon, would be born an American citizen.

In November Gabriela arrived with her children, Mariana and Fortunato, together with Cosimero the *peón de estribo*, Don Tomás's bookkeeper and other retainers. The party, traveling in wagons, was escorted to the border by fifty armed Yaqui Indians. Six days after Gabriela reached Bosque, her sixth child was born, a girl whom she named Anita. She never lost her belief that this child was the reincarnation of the baby she had miscarried the previous Christmas, during the turbulence created by the visit of the Tomochitecos.

Chapter Fifteen

WHEN CRUZ CHÁVEZ and his band of Tomochitecos returned to their village in February of 1892, they did so with full knowledge that they were, in the eyes of the government, dangerous rebels. The men were faced with two alternatives: submit or resist. Chávez knew the consequences of giving themselves over to the federal authorities. He and several other leaders would be shot and the remainder of the men deported to Yucatán as convict slave laborers; or they would be conscripted into the army. In the latter event, the dead leaders would be the fortunate ones.

If they resisted, Chávez decided, Tomochic would have a chance to survive. He knew the mountain villages were seething with unrest—they all feared that the *Ley Lerdo* would be invoked. On the journey to Cabora, Chávez had stopped to talk with Mayo and Yaqui warriors. Both groups were on the brink of violent insurrection. From Zacatecas, Morelos and Oaxaca, rumors came to him of discontent, of the masses chafing under the Díaz yoke. A spirited resistance by Tomochic could be the tiny flame that would ignite a widespread conflagration.

Cruz spent much time in prayer and deliberation inside the small, private chapel of his house. Above the simple altar hung a letter from Teresita, encased in a crudely carved frame. Its contents offered no suggestion of revolution, but dwelled instead on her unshakable faith in love and good works. Cruz read and re-read the letter daily, gaining strength and encouragement from his interpretation of her words. Wrought up by the momentous decision at hand, he sometimes engaged in allegorical reveries. To him, Teresita was a symbol of all that was good, pure and unselfish. She was surrounded by evil, greed and selfishness. She shone with the beauty of a gleaming pearl among dark brambles. If only the malevolent brambles could be plucked from the earth and destroyed! Her plight was similar to that of Tomochic. He and his people were oppressed by the same forces, whose greed for power must be stamped out. Such musings spurred him in his grim determination to resist to the utmost, for Teresita's sake as well as for that of his own village.

Chávez depended upon trusted spies at Guerrero and Piños Altos to keep him informed of the government's intentions and movements. In Guerrero his informant was Bernardo, the drunken half-brother of "San José." A clever dissembler, Bernardo was never so drunk that he forgot the nature of his mission. Affecting a glazed, stupid stare, weaving and staggering, he loitered about the federal garrison, where he was tolerated as a harmless sot. No one noticed his proclivity for stationing himself in locations where he could overhear conversations among the officers.

In August 1892 Cruz Chávez received information that the government was organizing a campaign to destroy Tomochic, as an example to all mountain villages entertaining thoughts of sedi-tion. Two armies, one from the east under General José Maria Rangel and one from the west under Colonel Lorenzo Torres, were to converge on the village.

Chávez called a meeting of his people at the church. After offering solemn prayers and hymns, he informed them of the impending attack. The time had come, he said, to make the crit-ical decision. The people could either submit or resist. He set forth anew the hazards of either course. Then he launched into a rousing speech, urging resistance to the last man.

"Even though Porfirio Díaz sends ten thousand bayonets against us, with the help of our beloved Santa de Cabora we will triumph over the Hosts of Hell!" he concluded, with his clenched fist raised in a mighty gesture of defiance. The Tomochitecos were vehement in their support.

Several nights later, General Rangel with his two hundred fifty troops camped on the Hill of the Cross overlooking the Valley of Tomochic. Cruz knew that Torres was still at Piños Altos, and presumed that Rangel would wait for the other officer. But Chávez was shrewd enough not to take chances.

A vain man, eager for military glory, Rangel was sure that his four-to-one advantage would guarantee an easy victory. He rashly decided not to wait for Torres. On September 1, therefore, he ordered an assault on Tomochic. Chávez and sixty Tomochitecos were waiting in the open outside the village. The federals approached on the double. As they advanced, they heard the Tomochitecos repeatedly shouting, "Long live the Saint of Cabora!" When they came within range, the Tomochitecos fired their first volley. The effect on Rangel's forces was deadly. For several minutes the din of battle was deafening. The superiority of the Tomochitecos' powerful, repeating Winchesters over the smooth-bore, single-shot Mausers of the federals more than offset the numerical advantage of the government troops. Rangel also failed to gauge the character of both his enemy and his own troops: the Tomochitecos were determined, dedicated men, imbued with religious zeal, whereas the federals were conscripts from all parts of Mexico, men whose secret sympathy was with the villagers they had been ordered to exterminate.

When the smoke cleared, one Tomochiteco had been killed, but the federals counted twenty-seven killed, fifty-one—including the wounded—taken prisoners, and the remainder scattered into the hills. General Rangel and his staff narrowly escaped capture. Among the wounded federal prisoners was Lieutenant Colonel Ramírez. All the prisoners were confined for the next two months in the *cuartelito*, a stone building near the house of Cruz Chávez.

When the report of Rangel's defeat reached Mexico City, Torres was ordered to remain at Piños Altos until a new army could be sent from Guerrero. Press censorship of the skirmish was absolute; no account of this disaster ever appeared in the Mexican newspapers.

After the battle, the Tomochitecos gathered at the church—not for celebration, but for thanksgiving to God and to La Santa, who received due credit for the victory. Chávez and his men were convinced that the calm following this battle was but an interlude before another assault by more powerful forces. The hours were spent in renewed dedication and preparation for the next encounter.

A few days later, Chávez sent word to Guerrero requesting that a doctor be sent to Tomochic to treat the wounded prisoners in the *cuartelito*. Dr. Francisco Arellano came for a day and did what he could, but some of the wounded refused to accept his services. They preferred the healing qualities of soap and water and of earth brought back from Cabora.

Even after treatment by the doctor, however, Lieutenant Colonel Ramírez's wound would not heal. On October 15 Ramírez asked for a conference with Chávez. When the Tomochiteco leader arrived at the *cuartelito*, the officer said, "Without constant and careful medical attention, I will slowly die. I want you either to have me shot immediately or allow me to go to the doctor in Guerrero."

Cruz called a meeting of his council, and all agreed to release the lieutenant colonel and furnish him with a horse for the ride to Guerrero. Chávez explained to the officer that he was being given his liberty because it was Santa Teresa's birthday. Moved by the wounded man's courage, the Tomochitecos treated him with profound respect and sympathy. When Ramírez was ready to depart, Chávez lined up all of his available men and invited the officer to review them. Ramírez was so touched by the gesture that, instead of the customary military review, he walked down the line shaking hands warmly with every man. As he passed, the

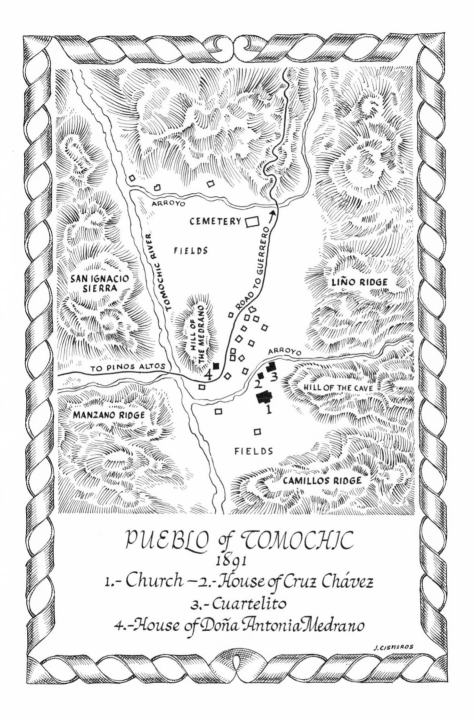

PUEBLO of TOMOCHIC
1891
1.- Church — 2.- House of Cruz Chávez
3.- Cuartelito
4.- House of Doña Antonia Medrano

J. CISNEROS

lieutenant colonel counted the defenders of Tomochic. All together there were one hundred five men.

The first chilly winds of fall in that high elevation were blowing from the northern sierras when Bernardo sent word that Rangel was again on his way to Tomochic, this time with an army three times the size of his previous forces. Torres was also on the march from Piños Altos with five hundred troops.

Chávez again called a convocation, making it mandatory for every person in the village to be at the church. The stone building was packed, as it always was when all of the three hundred twenty people of the community were present. Chávez conducted the service, all in the vernacular, somewhat after the fashion of a frontier Methodist circuit rider. He led the singing and did the praying and preaching. His prayer, extemporaneous and focused on the crisis at hand, was stirring and eloquent. From the Vulgate chapter of Second Kings, he read the story of how the Hosts of the King of Samaria besieged Israel and reduced its people to starvation. It was then that the power of God prevailed through the intercession of His servant Elisha. During the night, God caused the Hosts of Samaria to hear a noise of chariots and thundering horses. Thinking the Hittites had come to aid the Israelites, the Samarians fled in panic. Chávez applied the analogy to what he foresaw would happen at Tomochic. The Sons of Lucifer would come from the west and from the east and besiege the village. The Tomochitecos had their Santa de Cabora, God's living servant, to intercede for them. The fact that she was in Arizona Territory did not matter. She could "see things" at great distances and would sustain them in their time of need. They would triumph over the Hosts of Hell.

Chávez was magnificent—never had his powers of oratory been more inspired. Indomitable, his eyes flashing and his voice resounding to the rafters, he whipped the emotions of his people almost to the breaking point. Then, suddenly, he ceased to speak. A portentous silence ensued. With a change of manner, he looked fiercely at his followers as though singling out each and every man.

"If there is one among you of faint heart and little faith in the power of God and our Saint of Cabora, let him gather his family and depart from our village. We will not need you. We will be stronger without you."

After giving his message a few minutes to take hold and pointedly scanning the entire audience for signs of cowardice, he lowered his voice.

"Now, let us kneel for the Benediction."

The next day several families packed such belongings as they could carry and set off for other villages. Remaining with Cruz were sixty-eight male defenders, including boys over thirteen.

On October 20, 1892, the two armies arrived almost simultaneously. Rangel camped again on the Hill of the Cross to one side of Tomochic. Torres and his men positioned themselves in the Valley of the Spiders about two miles on the other side.

The next morning, Chávez climbed to the tower of the church and scanned the landscape in both directions. He could see the preparations for battle, and instantly made his own, anticipating the uncoordinated attack to follow. Torres, perhaps wishing credit this time for a victory, assaulted first without waiting for Rangel. Cruz sent all of his men to meet Torres. As before, the Winchesters were devastating. The entire command of Torres was thrown into confusion and retreated wildly back to the Valley of the Spiders. The carnage might have been even greater had Chávez allowed his men to follow; but realizing that Rangel would soon be attacking from the other direction, he recalled his forces.

The order came none too soon. Scarcely had the Tomochitecos regrouped when Rangel's troops were seen coming down the Hill of the Cross on the run. The battle was remarkably similar to that of the September skirmish with one exception: the federals did not scatter. Instead they retreated in one direction, but in hopeless disorder. A few miles from Tomochic, Rangel stopped the retreat. The rest of the day his men spent in camp, recovering. That night, by a roundabout march, Torres joined forces with Rangel.

Rangel also sent to Guerrero for additional conscripts, increasing his force to fifteen hundred soldiers in order to capture a village guarded by fewer than seventy. Now he moved with great caution. From the tower of the church, Chávez watched him enter the Valley of Tomochic at the northern end, carefully keeping behind him a small mesa called the Hill of the Medrano, which jutted from the valley floor. The Tomochitecos had taken up defensive positions in the church, in Chávez's house, and on the Hill of the Cave, a promontory just behind and overlooking the church.

The little war degenerated into a battle of attrition. Each day Chávez assessed the strategy of Rangel, as the officer deployed and extended his territory, gradually tightening his grip and closing in on the pockets of resistance. He cut the villagers off from their only water supply, the Tomochic River along the edge of the valley, and spent two days taking the Hill of the Cave, defended by twelve men. This single objective cost the federal armies some two hundred casualties. During each lull in the fighting, the hoarse battle cries of the Tomochitecos rang out: "Long live the Saint of Cabora" and "Long live the great power of God."

With the loss of the hill, Chávez had only his own house and the church left to defend. Over his house waved the flag of Tomochic, a white banner emblazoned with "La Santa de Cabora" in red letters. It had been embroidered by the village women.

All was quiet on the morning of the eighth day of the siege. For the first time in days there was no intermittent rifle fire, no booming of the Hotchkiss cannon. Rangel had tried to blast holes in the church, but the rifle shots from the tower forced the small cannon to remain at a sufficient distance to make its fire ineffective. By this time, Rangel had snipers concealed in empty houses controlling the open spaces between the house of Chávez and the church. Movement between the two buildings was impossible.

Barricaded within his house, Chávez was mystified by the lull in the battle, yet convinced that Rangel was up to some new trick. Peering with red and tired eyes through the portholes, he could see that the men in the church tower were also bewildered. The church had thick stone walls, a wooden roof, and a belfry just large enough for eight men. The defenders stationed there cautiously scanned the area for signs of trouble. All was disturbingly quiet at Rangel's camp on the Hill of the Medrano. About mid-morning Chávez saw a hundred or more troops move across the valley and climb the hills to the west. Later he watched them return, each carrying a bundle of faggots on his back. Chávez assumed that the sticks were to be used for firewood, and gave the activity no further thought. Still he searched his mind for every tactic the federals could be planning against him.

About mid-afternoon, Cruz perceived the full enormity of Rangel's strategy, and seethed with rage. A company of federals on the Hill of the Cave kept up a continuous rifle fire at the church belfry, forcing the defenders to keep their heads down. Soldiers carrying bundles of tinder ran toward the church, staying to the opposite side, out of range of Chávez's rifles. These men were followed by others carrying containers of oil. The bundles were stacked against the massive entrance door, the pile reaching to the roof. Chávez and his followers watched helplessly as oil was poured on the dried faggots and the pyre ignited.

Rigid with dread, the men inside the Chávez house watched the flames spread to the top of the dry tinder. As the heat increased, an updraft caused the fire to lick madly at the roof of the church, while an east wind sent the hungry flames racing to consume the wooden shingles. The entire roof was enveloped in one seething mass of angry flame, propelling billows of putrid gray smoke. Soon chunks of roof began to crumble into the church, carrying the inferno to the floor below.

Suddenly the church doors, now a fiery mass of lurid light,

burst open. Before the horrified eyes of Cruz and his people, the women of the village rushed out, dragging their children through the bed of scorching embers lying before the doors. They could hear the choking cries of the women and the terrified screams of the children as they ran barefoot across the burning coals. Unknown to the fleeing villagers, General Rangel had ordered the soldiers behind the churchyard wall to shoot down all who turned toward the Chávez house and to take as prisoners those who ran toward the federal troops. Those who scurried toward the house were shot to death; the few who turned toward the federal soldiers were captured. But not all the dead could be seen by those who watched from Chávez's house. Two days later General Rangel's men removed sixty-five charred, disfigured bodies from the debris inside the fire-blackened walls of the church.

That night was one of anguish for those still alive in the house of Cruz Chávez. They had been without water for three days. Moaning fitfully, women and children sprawled on the floor in various degrees of consciousness. Cruz, leaning against a wall near a porthole, heard his name called. Cautiously he looked out, but he could see nothing in the darkness.

"Who's there?" he called softly.

"It is Chabole, your old compadre."

Chávez recognized the voice of a Yaqui Indian he knew well. They had once gone on an expedition together, looking for the lost Torocote mine. Now he recalled that Chabole had been conscripted into the federal army. "What do you want, Chabole?"

"To save you. The night is dark. I know a way to lead you and the others through the federal lines. By morning you can be scattered safely among other villages."

Cruz considered the plan. "No, Chabole. It cannot be done. Many of our men are badly wounded. They cannot travel, and their women will not leave them. We, who are able to stand, cannot desert them. A thousand thanks for your offer."

"Then what can I do for you?"

"Water! Bring water!" Cruz opened the door and gave the

Indian a large earthen pot. Chabole brought the water and quickly turned to leave, repelled by the stench of decomposing bodies from within the crowded house. Some of them had been lying there for a week.

The following morning Rangel surrounded the house with several hundred riflemen, taking cover behind the ruins of the church and other vacant houses close by. These troops poured heavy fire at the portholes from every side. A few shots came from within, and then no more. Although the federals did not yet know it, the defenders had fired their last bullet. Soon the troops ceased firing altogether and ran in small groups toward the house, burdened with tinder, oil, mattocks and axes. At the wall, the soldiers made human ladders so that others could climb on their shoulders to the roof. The deadly supplies were passed to those on top, who then cut holes through the flat roof, poured oil on the bundles of sticks, set them afire, and dropped the flaming tinder into the rooms of the house. The floors and walls were of earth and stone, and there was little below that would ignite. So the fires were fed from above with saturated sticks. Each hole became a chimney, belching forth black pillars of smoke.

With a battering ram, the soldiers broke down the front door and rushed inside to find their victims blind and helpless from the smoke and fire. So dense were the fumes that the federals could remain inside only for a minute or so. One by one they dragged out those defenders who seemed still alive. Of these there were seven men, all wounded. The last to emerge was Chávez, supported by his sister-in-law, Doña Clara Calderón. Wounded in both legs, one arm hanging limp, the proud leader dragged his rifle with his good hand.

Reviving slightly in the fresh air, Chávez stood unsteadily, leaning on his useless rifle. He asked for a cigarette, and as he smoked it, Doña Clara was ordered to go to federal headquarters and bring back a military doctor for the wounded. She shuffled off hopefully, but before she had reached the hill, a volley of rifle fire cracked the stillness. She knew she had been betrayed, and turning back, saw all seven of the last defenders lying dead before the firing squad. The giant body of Cruz lay where he had fallen, on top of his brother David, his beard thrust defiantly into the air.

Of the original population of Tomochic, not a man or boy over thirteen survived the siege. The sixty-nine male defenders had held out, with no hope of rescue, for ten days against odds of twenty-three to one.

During the next two days, General Rangel added the finishing touches to his complete destruction of the village. A few wooden houses, close in and protected by the Tomochiteco rifles, had not been burned. These were torn down and the wood used for funeral pyres. The dead were stacked on the pyres like so much cordwood and reduced to ashes in the leaping flames. Pains were taken to see that the body of Chávez was placed on top. Then the stone houses and earthen houses were demolished, all except that of the turncoat Reyes Domínguez, whose dwelling was left alone among the rubble. At the far end of the village, the lonely ruins of the church rose starkly against the smoke-darkened sky.

Anxious to conceal the greed and political scheming that led to the rebellion, the Díaz government blamed the uprising on the seditious influence of Teresa Urrea. Because letters from Teresita to Chávez were found in the rebel's house, reports were circulated that she had been in constant communication with the leaders of the revolt. But the government never revealed the contents of these letters.

Captain Francisco Castro, who was directed to search the house of Chávez for evidence concerning the rebellion, found the letters, miraculously undamaged, in Cruz's office-chapel. Before turning them over to General Rangel he read them. In the book *Peleandro en Tomochic*, published in 1957, Castro described their contents: "She recommended tolerance and love for one's neighbors, aid for the destitute, mercy by the victors, and succor for the dying. She said Charity is the best road to God.

At no place in the famous letters did she incite rebellion in any manner. The contents of the letters were clear, and in no way could anything she said be interpreted as inspiring violence. The letters revealed the author as a contemplative person, possessed of extraordinary spirituality."

Castro further stated that the unwavering courage of the Tomochitecos in the cause of freedom for the mestizos and Indians produced an indelible, sympathetic impression on the soldiers who destroyed them. Almost to a man, they later joined the cause for which the tenacious mountain men, inspired by their Saint of Cabora, had given their lives. Castro himself helped overthrow the Díaz regime. Years later Tomochic became a symbol for the Mexican Revolution of 1910. Francisco Madero, its leader, considered the little rebellion "the most heroic and dedicated instance of Mexican valor."

And in his *Episodios Mexicanos* Mario Gill wrote: "Of all the crimes of the Porfirio Díaz regime the most monstrous was against the village in the sierras of western Chihuahua, Tomochic. . . . Apart from the heroism of the men of Tomochic, which is like a page out of the history of Sparta, there was a singular and extraordinary factor. This was the inspiration of a nineteen-year-old girl, Teresa Urrea, whom they called La Santa de Cabora. Her name was their battle cry, and was on the lips of the Tomochitecos unto the death of the last man."

Chapter Sixteen

THE TRAGEDY OF TOMOCHIC left Teresita stunned. She remained in a semi-trance for days, her thoughts turning inward. The family, whose newly arrived members had brought the news, feared that another cataleptic state was imminent. Gradually, awareness of the waiting sick and afflicted aroused her. Gravely, almost grimly, her compassion for the ailing overcame her grief, and she resumed her ministrations. Months passed before she was herself again. Often a shadow that came from within caused her smile to fade.

Lauro Aguirre, now newly incensed by Tomochic, again urged her to join the revolutionary crusade. Tomochic, he said, could be utilized as the fall of the Alamo had been used in the Texas Revolution of 1836, when Houston's inspired citizen army made short shrift of General Santa Ana and his conscripts at San Jacinto. Aguirre argued and pleaded, but Teresita adhered steadfastly to her doctrine of nonviolence.

Disappointed by her unwavering stance, Aguirre returned to Nogales. His revolutionary campaign with *El Progresista* was going none too well. The class of Indians and Mexicans to whom he appealed could not read, and he was unable to make any impression on American opinion. So far as the United States was concerned, the tragic affair of Tomochic had never happened, in spite of the news stories. The one factor needed to spark the movement, Aguirre knew, was the active participation of Teresita. Having failed to achieve this, he decided to implicate her indirectly by association.

Lauro secured a photograph of her, had a plate made, and on smooth paper ran off prints by the tens of thousands in his shop. The picture portrayed Teresita seated behind a table with one elbow resting lightly upon it, her fingers touching her left cheek. Her abundant hair flowed over her shoulders like a dark veil, framing a serene face with eyes looking directly at the viewer —a startling, Madonna-like effect. Across the bottom was the caption:

Teresa Urrea

La Santa de Cabora

La Espíritu de Tomochic

The leaders of the malcontents passed out copies to pilgrims from Mexico. No restrictions at this time prevented the Mexican people from coming and going across the United States-Mexican border at will. The pictures were treasured as sacred mementos by Teresita's followers. Men placed them in their shirt pockets, over their hearts, and women mounted them above the crude altars in their homes.

For three years Don Tomás had watched with misgivings the growth of the revolutionary activities centering around Bosque and Nogales. He had not received his final citizenship certificate, and he worried that he would be identified with an international movement, thus jeopardizing his naturalization. Although he had ample personal reasons for wishing the overthrow of Porfirio Díaz, he was also fearful of what a revolution would mean to his people and to the *hacendados* of Mexico. Their estates might be divided and given to the peons. His family by Doña Loreto would lose its inheritance. Furthermore, the ranches were still the sole support for himself, Teresita and Gabriela's family. There was nothing he could do to stop the movement, but he could not sanction a revolution. He must, at all costs, safeguard his Mexican interests and his chances of obtaining American citizenship. His three probationary years were almost over. To make sure no disqualifying incident occurred, he decided to move his family farther back into the interior of Arizona.

One day a delegation arrived from San José, Arizona, a village on the Gila River, five miles above Solomonville, a hundred sixty miles northeast of Bosque. A very well-known cripple in San José had been cured by Teresita, and the community was anxious to have her move to its village. The citizens would furnish a house and send a caravan of covered wagons to move the entire household. Don Tomás, implementing his resolve, accepted the offer.

At San José, the number of pilgrims arriving from Mexico to see Teresita decreased considerably because of the isolation of the place. The reduced number of Mexican patients, however, was in a measure compensated for by the Spanish-speaking people who came from all parts of Arizona and New Mexico. Teresita's beneficent practice continued undiminished.

After the departure of the Urrea family, Lauro Aguirre moved his family to El Paso, Texas, taking the staff and press for *El Progresista* with him. Eight months after Don Tomás had settled in San José, Aguirre arrived from El Paso to persuade his old friend to move to that city. What inducements he offered no one can say. But Don Tomás, now a fully naturalized citizen of the United States and no longer in fear of extradition, consented. After moving his household to Texas via the Southern Pacific Railroad, Don Tomás rented a large brick house on Mesa Street, at that time the fashionable residential section of El Paso. As news of Teresita's arrival spread across the river to Juárez, the street filled with Mexicans from both sides of the Río Grande. The crowds around the Urrea house became a familiar sight to the residents of El Paso. Teresita later told a reporter that during her residence in that city she saw about two hundred patients a day. She also mentioned a number of men who came from many places to ask her to marry them, but her father always refused his consent. Nor had she any wish to marry any of them, she said.

In the meantime, the *El Paso Times* and other newspapers carried photographs and numerous interviews and news stories about her good works. The merchants quickly discovered that Teresita was good for business. One citizen observed that "it looks as if half the people in Las Cruces, New Mexico, are in town every day." Local businessmen erected a large tent on a vacant lot near the Urrea house so that patients and pilgrims could wait with some protection from the weather.

The Urrea family found El Paso a pleasant place to live, and Teresita was happy with the increased opportunities for doing her work. Aguirre proposed that she join him as co-author of a book on the destruction of Tomochic. He had now changed the name of *El Progresista* to *El Independiente*. His plan was to run the story first as a serial in his newspaper, hold the type, and reprint it in book form. Teresita agreed on condition that the publication be dedicated to the faith and heroism of Cruz Chávez and his courageous Tomochitecos. Aguirre agreed to her stipulation, secretly hoping that keeping the memory of Tomochic alive would aid the cause of the revolution.

The articles appeared—Aguirre doing the actual writing—and the book was published. While the work was still in progress, Aguirre quietly made periodic trips by railroad to Nogales, where he conspired with revolutionary leaders. Then, on August 13, 1896, an Aguirre-inspired invasion of Mexico was launched by Mexican nationals operating from points along the borders of Arizona, New Mexico and Texas. The revolutionists called themselves the "Teresistas."

The attack began at 3:30 that morning when some sixty Yaqui Indians, shouting "Viva Santa Teresa" and "Viva la Santa de Cabora," besieged the Mexican customs house at Nogales on the Sonora side of the international boundary. Armed with assorted guns, bows and arrows, machetes and axes, the Yaquis quickly dispatched the guards and took over the customs house. Gunshots aroused the townspeople on both sides of the barbed wire fence separating the towns of Nogales, Arizona Territory, from Nogales, Sonora. American citizens, suspecting the return of bank robbers, commandeered all available firearms, including forty militia guns from the armory. Crossing the border, they joined in the fight against the Indians. The battle that followed lasted several hours, during which time seven Indians were killed, one wounded, and one taken prisoner. Four Mexicans, including the two guards, were also killed, and many others were injured. After daylight, the citizens and officers defended Nogales with such force that the Indians retreated to the hills south of Nogales, Sonora, made a roundabout march, crossed the border into Arizona Territory, and dispersed. The Mexican authorities discovered that each of the fallen Yaquis had carried one of Aguirre's prints of Teresita over his heart.

That same day attacks were made on every Mexican customs house from Nogales to Ojinaga, across the border from Presidio, Texas. Not even in one town were the insurgents able to hold their positions for more than a few hours. The attempt on Juárez failed completely, because of the strength of the federal garrison there. By nightfall the entire "revolution" had collapsed.

Lauro Aguirre sadly put forth his reasons for the failure, foremost of which was the refusal of Teresita to sanction the attempt. Had she given the cause her blessing or, even better, had she mounted a horse and placed herself at the head of a column, tens of thousands of Indians and mestizos would have rushed to join her. Aguirre was also vexed by the refusal of the United States government to offer material aid or armed forces. The American people, he was convinced, regarded Mexico as a frontier for American enterprise and exploitation. They had no quarrel with the dictator who was helping them to realize handsome profits.

The Teresistas went underground for fourteen years; those

who were left in 1910 joined Francisco Madero in a massive movement against the dictator, forcing Porfirio Díaz to flee the country and take refuge in Paris.

In 1896, the Díaz government blamed Teresita for the "invasions" of August 13. In Washington the Mexican ambassador demanded that she be extradited to Mexico for trial. When his request was denied, he insisted that she be forceably removed from the border. The United States Department of State promised to see to the matter.

Within this same period, Don Tomás stated, three separate attempts were made on Teresita's life. The assailants were probably either agents of Díaz or fanatical followers of Father Gustelúm, or both. The *patrón* arranged for her to be guarded day and night, and kept a constant watch on her himself. Since Texas law prohibited him from wearing pistols, he carried a Winchester and wore a belt of cartridges at all times. He was thus armed when a United States marshal called at the house and explained that the State Department would be saved great embarrassment if Don Tomás would move his household, including Teresita, back into the interior at least a hundred miles from the border. Don Tomás replied that he was already considering such a move.

Teresita's father chose Clifton, Arizona, because he had visited there while the family was at San José. He had liked the town for its natural beauty, reminiscent of Alámos, as well as for its bustling mining activities. He acquired a few acres of land with several small houses in the narrow valley in the lower part of town, just north of the San Francisco River. The location was sufficiently remote to discourage agents of the Mexican government and religious fanatics with designs on Teresita's life. One of the houses was enlarged for the family residence, leaving the smaller houses free for the family retainers.

After living in town only a few weeks, Don Tomás discovered that two items—milk and firewood—were extremely scarce. In part to augment his income from the ranches in Mexico and also to keep from being bored, he started a dairy and a woodyard.

For the wood business, he employed fifteen to twenty Mexicans and purchased some fifty donkeys. Teams of men and burros scoured the almost barren mountainsides for miles around, gathering the scrubby juniper growth that furnished fragrant fires for the hearths of Clifton and nearby Morenci. Both the dairy and firewood ventures proved profitable.

Teresita's half-sister, Anita Urrea Treviño, remembered this period as idyllic: "Those were happy days. Illustrious and educated people came from as far away as Mexico City and New York to see Teresita. My father's household never knew how many people there would be for dinner, or to spend the night. Teresita was always gay when not working with the sick. She was the life of the place. She played the marimbas and the guitar, and sang in her rich, melodious voice. I remember well how she charmed everyone."

The move to Clifton marked a change in Teresita's work. Because of the town's isolation and relatively small population, the demands made on her were greatly reduced. Soon, however, the more prominent citizens became interested in what she was doing for the families of the mineworkers. A frequent visitor to the Urrea home, and an interested observer of Teresita's treatments, was Dr. L. A. W. Burtch, the local physician. He did not understand how she did it, he said, but often she obtained results with some of the patients he himself had been unable to help. Most of these, he noted, were chronic and traumatic cases that did not respond to medical treatment. He began to refer such patients to her, and a lasting friendship developed between the two.

It was probably owing to Dr. Burtch's influence that Teresita was taken up by the wealthy members of the community: the bankers, the lawyers and the American and British mine owners. One of the bankers, C. P. Rosencrans, was the distraught father of a six-year-old boy who suffered from the paralyzing effects of a debilitating disease, possibly polio. When Dr. Burtch found that he could do nothing for the child's condition, he recommended that Teresita be allowed to treat the boy. In three weeks, the banker's son showed a marked improvement, and the Anglo members of the Clifton community were greatly impressed.

In October of 1899 the peaceful routine of Teresita's new existence was abruptly shattered. A worker in one of the mines fell in love with the handsome young woman. There was certainly nothing unusual about a man losing his head over her. Many men had been suddenly and irresistibly attracted to her— even the Mexican general escorting her into exile. The strange difference this time was that Teresita herself was attracted to the young miner and convinced that she was in love with him. She had long affirmed that she intended to marry some day. And before leaving Cabora, she had predicted to Josefina Félix that the man she chose for a husband would be cruel to her, indeed would attempt to kill her.

Guadalupe Rodríguez, nicknamed "Lupe," was said to be half-Yaqui. Teresita's half-sisters remembered him as tall, fair and handsome. He must also have been very persuasive, with a manner as engaging as his appearance. Don Tomás, however, did not approve of him. He considered him a man of unstable character, not to be trusted, and forbade Rodríguez to set foot on his property.

On the morning of June 22, 1900, Don Tomás was sitting on the veranda of his house. Suddenly Lupe appeared, carrying a carbine. He pointed the gun at Don Tomás and demanded his permission to marry Teresita. Don Tomás emphatically told Lupe his opinion of him. The young man stormed at his unyielding opponent, and then left precipitately. Had this occurred at Cabora, Don Tomás would probably have horse-whipped or shot the man, as a matter of *hacendado* justice. But he was in Arizona, where there was considerable anti-Mexican prejudice; and he had determined to abide strictly by local laws. In an hour Rodríguez was back with a justice of the peace, a Mexican-American friend of his. Pointedly flourishing the carbine, Lupe demanded that he and Teresita be married there and then.

At that moment Teresita appeared, torn between relief that she could act decisively and anguish for the father she adored and must leave. With an imploring look at her father, she walked to Lupe's side and stated to the justice of the peace that she was twenty-seven years old and it was her will to marry this man. The justice read the ceremony as Don Tomás, his face contorted in an expression of sorrow and rage, helplessly looked on.

Teresita gathered together some of her clothes and went with Lupe to his house in Metcalf, a town up Ward Canyon, about five miles from Clifton. She later testified in a Los Angeles court that a number of her friends followed them to Metcalf, and the entire night was spent in dancing and merrymaking. The marriage was not consummated.

The next morning Rodríguez acted surly and distant. He tore up some of his bride's belongings and packed her clothes into a bundle. Grabbing the carbine and slinging the bundle over his shoulder, he ordered Teresita to follow him.

"Come, Teresa, we will now go to Mexico."

"I dare not," she protested. "You know they would kill me in Mexico."

He seized her hands, to lead her to the station. Teresita's friends, alarmed by his bullying manner, begged her not to go with him. With no knowledge of where he was going but still under his spell, she followed him out of the house and along the railroad tracks. After walking in silence for some time, Lupe started to run. She ran after him but he soon outdistanced her. Suddenly he turned and shot, barely missing her. At once he turned again, and ran up into the hills.

Teresita's friends, following at a distance, caught up with her and escorted her, shaken and weeping, back to her father's house in Clifton. A posse of two hundred men went after Rodríguez and found him late that day. Lupe resisted savagely until all his cartridges were gone. Then the men, overpowering him, carried him back to Clifton and put him in the jail, an old mine tunnel with bars over the opening.

That evening, Teresita went to see him.

"I am sure you would not have acted so if you loved me," she said sadly.

"I don't love you," Lupe screamed, shaking the bars of his cell. "I hate you. When I get out of here I will follow you, no matter where you are, and kill you!"

A few days later he was tried, found insane, and sent to an asylum. The marriage had lasted exactly one day.

Four years later Teresita obtained a divorce in California. At the hearing, she testified that she and her father had become convinced that Rodríguez was an agent of the Díaz government, hired to bring her back to Mexico, and that this was where he had intended to take her the day after the wedding. In the event that abduction proved too difficult, he was to produce evidence that she was dead and no longer a threat to the government. He could then claim his reward. A number of statements made by Rodríguez during his rational moments in the Clifton jail supported these suspicions. On one occasion he mumbled something of his kidnapping plans to the sheriff. On another he told a deputy that he was not worried, that General Díaz would see to his extradition.

Back in her father's house, Teresita realized how deeply her sudden marriage had wounded Don Tomás. She could not look at him without seeing the hurt in his eyes and sensing his disappointment in her actions. When, a few days after her return, Mrs. Rosencrans offered to take her to California to treat the sick child of one of her friends, Teresita readily agreed to go. The trauma of her brief marriage and the rift with her father convinced Teresita that it would be better to leave Clifton for a while.

More than five hundred people, according to the Clifton newspaper, gathered at the railroad station to see Teresita on her way. Women were weeping; men were misty-eyed. As the train pulled out, the crowd was a sea of waving handkerchiefs. Teresita stood on the rear platform, tears running down her cheeks, not looking at the crowd, but with her eyes fixed on Don Tomás, who stood apart, rigidly erect and silent. She never saw him again.

In San José, California, Teresita visited the three-year-old daughter of Mrs. Fessler, and within weeks the sick child, who had not responded to the attentions of five medical doctors, showed remarkable improvement. The newspapers seized on the dramatic cure, and took to their hearts the young woman who had effected it. All the major dailies, including *The San Francisco Examiner, The Chronicle* and *The Call*, sent reporters to interview Teresita. The resulting articles and photographs attracted much attention, and led to a proposition by a so-called "medical company" to sponsor Teresita and make her ministrations available to people throughout the United States. The company would pay her $2000 a year for five years. The officers of the company gave Teresita assurances that their enterprise was a philanthropic organization interested only in making her services available gratis to the public. No patient would ever be charged for her services. The $2000 offered her, they explained, represented compensation for her expenses and was not intended as salary.

Had she been able to confer with her father, Teresita probably would have been deterred from accepting the company's proposal. As it was, she found herself independent for the first time. The company, she reasoned, offered the means by which she could continue to perform her good works. Teresita signed the contract.

With vague promises of sending her to Europe, India, and even to Egypt, the company officials launched Teresita on a United States tour lasting four years. In St. Louis, Missouri, where she stayed for several months, she found herself handicapped by an inability to speak English well, and searched the city for a suitable interpreter. When no one could be located, Teresita wrote to a close and trusted friend, Mrs. Juana Van Order, in Solomonville, Arizona, asking her to send one of her sons to St. Louis to act as interpreter. Mrs. Van Order's two sons— John, nineteen, and Harry, eighteen—were both bilingual. She herself was a mestiza Mexican, whose Dutch husband had died in 1899. Teresita had met Juana Van Order when the Urreas lived near Solomonville, and had found her an intelligent and highly respected person. The friendship between the two women had blossomed during Teresita's years in Arizona and developed into a relationship of great mutual affection. Next to Mariana, Juanita was her closest confidante.

When she received Teresita's request, Juana Van Order immediately sent her nineteen-year-old son, John, to help her friend communicate with the English-speaking patients. Written communications at the time were scant and far between, and no one knows what happened after John arrived. A few months later, however, news came to Clifton that John and Teresita were "married" (though the divorce from Rodríguez would not be official for some three years). Whether the alliance was a matter of convenience with respect to social conventions or a genuine attraction has never been made clear. Those who knew John Van Order at the time said that he was a strikingly handsome man, an assertion supported by contemporary photographs.

Soon after the marriage, Teresita and her traveling companions of the medical company arrived in New York City, where she settled for a few months in an apartment at 110 East 28th Street. Although the promoters of the company may have been wanting in integrity, they were well practiced in public relations. The newspapers gave Teresita extensive coverage. *The New York Journal* of March 3, 1901 devoted an entire page to the story, with three photographs and a seven-column headline: " 'Santa Teresa,' the fanatical Mexican 'Miracle Worker,' in New York."

By all accounts, the medical company did well in New York. Later John Van Order told his brother Harry that Teresita cured many wealthy people, who lavished expensive gifts on her. Always indifferent to worldly goods, Teresita gave these presents to the poor. But her husband was of a different turn of mind, and often expressed exasperation at Teresita's charitable instincts. If she would only use her abilities for profit, she would become a very wealthy woman, and they would both be handsomely supported for life.

In 1902 Teresita gave birth to a baby girl whom she named Laura, feminine for Lauro, after Aguirre. It was also during her tour of New York that Teresita received word of her father's death. Don Tomás had died of typhoid fever on September 22, 1902, and was buried in the Shannon Hill Cemetery of Clifton. The effect of this news on Teresita is not on record. No doubt it was traumatic, and may have been the reason for Teresita's insisting that the medical company leave New York and go to Los Angeles, where she remained for about a year and a half. In Los Angeles she became actively interested in the social and economic plight of the Mexican population of that city. Her concern for the poor and underpaid workers and their families caused considerable apprehension among the less sympathetic members of the Anglo-controlled economy and political system. The situation was reminiscent of those last years at Cabora when her solicitude for the Yaqui and Mayo tribes had also roused the animosity of the establishment. The Los Angeles sojourn was further made uneasy by her growing disillusionment with the promoters of the medical company.

The cruellest stroke of fortune in the year following her father's death occurred one sultry night in late August when a fire destroyed Teresita's little cottage on the corner of State Street and Brooklyn Avenue. She moved in with friends nearby. A few months later she discovered that she was pregnant again. Exhausted, she wrote to her mother-in-law that she wished to return to Arizona for the birth of her second child. Juana Van Order responded immediately. She urged her to come to her farm near Solomonville, and hurried to have two new rooms added to her house. In June 1904 Teresita arrived, and her second daughter, Magdalena, was born soon afterward.

Teresita had saved a considerable sum of money during her four years with the medical company. She bought a lot in Clifton and erected a large, two-story house with eight rooms. Her husband appears to have taken little interest in her plans at this time. While her new residence was under construction, she stayed with Gabriela in the house purchased by Don Tomás nine years earlier. All support from the ranches in Sonora had been withdrawn, and Gabriela was hard-pressed to maintain both the household and her brood of children. The strain of life had aged her visibly. The two women easily resumed their close companionship and spent many hours in delighted reminiscence about Don Tomás and life at Cabora. Teresita was happy to see the three youngest children, the last of whom had been born three months after Don Tomás's death.

When Teresita's house was finished, she furnished it in what was said by her contemporaries to be good taste. One room upstairs was called the "Flower Room" and was constructed so as to admit a maximum of sunlight. Here Teresita could grow flowers, one of her greatest delights, for they bloomed the entire year. In her new house, the Clifton newspaper reported, she "hoped to nurse the sick to health and to heal the wounds of the injured."

Chapter Seventeen

When Teresita returned to Clifton, Gabriela and other friends realized that she was a changed person. Moody and introspective, she seemed even to have lost some of her curing powers. No more did she play the guitar and sing. They blamed the change on something that must have happened during the four years of her association with the medical company. They knew she still grieved for Don Tomás. Teresita told them that she had been prevented from attending his last illness and funeral because of medical company commitments in New York. Her present moods could also be an aftermath, they speculated, or the result of her unwillingness and inability to adjust to the life demanded of her by the medical company and her husband.

A wise and perceptive man once said, "It takes the right kind of soil to grow a saint." The conditions were right at Cabora and in the border towns in Arizona and Texas, and even in Clifton. Here Teresita had been admired, adored, cherished and protected, and her powers respected. But when she came under the auspices of professional promoters, the climate grew cold, critical and unsympathetic. In effect, she was treated as just another faith healer. Her sensitive nature had never been able to adjust to such an atmosphere. Seeking refuge from those years of exploitation, she returned to Clifton and to the people who understood and loved her.

As the last pieces of furniture were moved into Teresita's new house, her health began to fail. She started to lose weight and tired easily. She was bothered by a persistent, hacking cough. At first she gave the symptoms little thought, believing that her condition was a result of too much strain and too little sleep. Now that she was back with her family in a town where she was respected by everyone, Teresita believed she would start mending and recover her old vigor. She had only to get settled in.

Weeks passed and Teresita's energy continued to diminish; her cheeks appeared hollow, her color pallid, and her eyes deeper set and more luminous. Dr. Burtch noticed the change, and had grave suspicions concerning its cause. At first, he hesitated to mention his concern. Then one day he spoke to her gently.

"Teresita, are you feeling well?"

She looked at him. "No. I am not well."

"Do you know why?"

"I believe I have lung trouble."

"Would you mind if I examined you?"

"Not at all."

Dr. Burtch completed his examination. Solemnly he shook his head. "It is lung trouble. The symptoms are unmistakable."

Teresita understood too well the gravity of his pronouncement, but was unperturbed. She smiled at him slightly.

"Do you have a remedy?"

"There is no remedy except plenty of rest and wholesome food."

"Yes, I know. It is true."

Swinging his stethoscope meditatively, Dr. Burtch walked back and forth across the room.

"Nature plays ironical tricks," he said at length. "Truly it's not fair for you who have cured tens of thousands to fall victim to this malady."

Teresita regarded him compassionately as if he were the

afflicted and she were giving consolation. "It doesn't matter. If it were not this sickness, it would be some other. Our Lord cured others but he did not save Himself."

Dr. Burtch marveled at her serenity. He had one further comment to add, but hesitated. He was not sure how she would take it.

"As you well know, this lung trouble is considered contagious. You should not see any more patients."

"I understand. I feel that my commitment to the Holy Mother is now fulfilled. She does not expect more of me." She saw that the doctor did not comprehend the "commitment to the Holy Mother," but she let it pass.

"May I ask a favor, Doctor?"

"Yes, of course."

"Let us not speak to anyone of my condition."

He nodded, and this was the last time they ever mentioned Teresita's illness, although Dr. Burtch continued to drop by regularly to visit her. He sent out word that Santa Teresa, as she was called in Clifton, was ill and would need absolute rest for a while. Teresita did not seem to miss her patients when they stopped coming.

She entered a period of resignation and serenity, and appeared exceedingly content. She still had some money, enough to last for a year or two. Mariana was in charge of the housekeeping again, and she cared for Teresita as though the grown woman were her own child. Just across the river was Gabriela's household of ten children, ranging in age from three to twenty, all of them devoted to their gentle half-sister. One or more of the children were at Teresita's house every day. They were always welcomed by their well-beloved Mariana, now a strikingly handsome woman of mature middle age, whose kindly face and soft brown eyes revealed warmth and intelligence. Ever since the day she had entered Cabora in an oxcart and walked out on her own two legs, cured of rheumatic fever, her loyalty to Teresita had never wavered. When Gabriela's children were there, Mariana would take them to the Flower Room, where Teresita was usually to be found, and they would talk, sometimes for hours.

Mariana was a spellbinding storyteller, one with imagination and a sense of the dramatic. One of Teresita's half-sisters, Marieta, who was about ten at the time, remembered how she used to slip into the room to listen while Mariana reminisced about her girlhood in Alámos or the more stirring and startling events in Teresita's life at Cabora, Bosque or El Paso. During these sessions, Teresita seemed to throw off the ravages of her malady; her features became animated, her eyes sparkled, and her merry laugh could be heard throughout the house.

Teresita was eager to hear of all that had taken place in Clifton while she was away. When Mariana once tried to question her in turn about her travels with the medical company, she became grave and evasive, giving the impression that she did not choose to talk or think about those events. Sensing her friend's reluctance to dredge up that part of her past, Mariana never broached the subject again. No one among Teresita's friends ever learned the details of her life during those years.

Except for Mariana, no member of the extended family took Teresita's illness seriously. Everyone assumed that she was over-worked and run down, and that rest and good food enjoyed among friends and family would soon restore her strength and vitality. Especially concerned over her loss of weight, the neighbors all sent tasty gifts to tempt her appetite. Nearly every housewife in Clifton prepared special dishes: delicate custards, meats, vegetables, many kinds of breads, cakes and pies from the Anglo-Americans, and all kinds of savory native dishes from the Latin-American households.

Teresita's favorite diversion during her illness was the care of her flowers. She grew geraniums, both the bush type in pots and the trailing variety, blooming in hanging baskets. Begonias, interspersed with asparagus ferns, added patterns of color before the many windows. Her favorite was a brilliant red hibiscus plant brought back from California.

Teresita had a way, as they said, with flowers: the plants were all responsive and vigorous. To her, each one had a personality. Sometimes she would talk softly to them, and they seemed to respond. The hibiscus put forth a blossom nearly every day in blooming season. A large, delicate and fragile flower of exquisite beauty, it lasted but a day and then withered and died. She compared the hibiscus to a sunflower, which was hardy and tough and would last many days. Yet, she meditated, the hibiscus with its delicate fragility produced more beauty in one short day than the sunflower does in many days. The thought occurred to her that the same could be true of people.

An occasion was made of Teresita's birthday on October 15, 1905. Well-wishers, Anglos and Spanish-speaking people, filed through her house all afternoon. Unable to stand, she received them sitting in a high-backed rocking chair. Many brought gifts, and when the party was over, the kitchen overflowed with food. One unusual feature of the reception went unnoticed at the time. As each guest left, Teresita uttered not the usual expression of departure, *"Hasta manāna"* or *"Hasta la vista"*—"until I see you again"—but *"Adios"*—"goodbye." Members of the family later recalled this, and were convinced that she bade each guest a final goodbye that day. More than once, even before leaving Cabora, she had predicted that she would die before she was thirty-three. They believed she knew that this would be her last birthday.

Her strength continued to diminish slowly. She stayed in bed longer each morning, and after a time she made no effort to get up until afternoon. She felt no pain, only a great physical languor. Her mind was clear and active. Since Teresita's relatives thought she should not be alone while she was awake, someone was always on hand to sit with her. Yet there were times when she much preferred to be alone. Often she pretended to be asleep when someone entered the room. Usually the visitor would tiptoe out, leaving Teresita with her thoughts.

Most often these thoughts turned to those who had helped her most. Don Tomás came repeatedly to mind; his staunch support, his acts of kindness and his unquestioning love were part of all her remembrances. He never believed that her cures were miracles or that she was a saint. She herself did not know how she had cured certain people, but she knew that her father was right about her not being a saint.

She wondered if Huila, her old friend, would have believed her to be a saint. She never recalled that wizened old woman without admiration for her wisdom, and gratitude for all she had done for the people of Cabora and for her. Huila was such a sensible old woman; she probably would have agreed with Don Tomás on the question of sainthood. She would have given all credit for the cures to the knowledge she had passed on to Teresita about herbs and people.

Occasionally she thought about the local Catholic Church and its priest. He had not come to see her and acted very aloof. She had been told that he was a young Spaniard, very rigid in his beliefs and distrustful of all unorthodox individuals and groups, including the Protestant sects. He probably considered her a heretic, since it was generally known that she herself had baptized a number of persons, most of them infants, before they had died.

Occasionally she recalled Lauro Aguirre, the only intellectual she had ever known well. He was still living in El Paso, publishing *El Independiente* and promoting the revolutionary cause. She speculated on what might have happened had she mounted a white horse in response to his urging and headed the "invasion" of Mexico in person in 1896. Her utmost sympathy was still with the Yaquis, the Mayos and the villages in the sierras, but bloodshed was not for her. The troubles of the world would never be solved by violence. They never had been, so far as she knew. Only love, tolerance and understanding could bring lasting peace. The memory of the beautiful lady who had spoken to her of love remained very vivid in her mind.

Cruz Chávez, for instance, was one who thought violence would solve the world's wrongs. She never recalled Cruz without being suffused by acute sadness. Such a giant of a man with such child-like faith and simplicity! Remembering their meeting and her letters to him, Teresita always regretted that her powers had not softened that stubborn rebel's implacable hatred. He had succeeded only in getting himself and his people killed. Now he was a martyr to his religion and a hero for the revolution.

Chávez's beliefs were shared by Don Lauro. He contended that some changes can only come about through strife and battle. He had written her that the chances for revolution were better than ever, that Cruz Chávez dead was worth more to the movement than a thousand Cruz Chávezes alive, and that Tomochic was now the symbol of the revolution. What was needed, he repeated, was a leader, and now at last there was a young man in Coahuila, Francisco Madero by name, who gave promise of becoming a national hero. Poor Don Lauro, he had finally given up his hopes for her.

Remembering Cabora, she was filled with an overpowering longing. Her happiest days had been spent there, and there her greatest work had been achieved. She repeatedly mused on the many incidents that had occurred in that place and the people who were involved. She could close her eyes and see the house with its long, shadowy verandas and high, carved corbels. She understood that Doña Loreto was now living at Cabora, and that she had never forgiven Teresita for all that had happened. All of Doña Loreto's children, except Tomás *hijo*, were married now, and Loreto was finding great pleasure in her fast-increasing collection of grandchildren. How fortunate those children were to be at Cabora!

During her more active moments, Teresita lavished much attention on her daughters, Laura, now three, and Magdalena, just beginning to walk. She controlled her constant impulse to hold them to her and cover them with kisses. Aware of the contagious character of her illness, she asserted strong self-discipline and kept them at a distance, entrusting their needs to Mariana and the nieces and nephews who might be around.

Her thoughts sometimes turned to John Van Order and to her relationship with him. When her good friend, Juana, had sent John to St. Louis to be her interpreter, her unconsummated but legal marriage to Guadalupe Rodríguez had still been in effect. Teresita's liaison with John, therefore, had not yet the status of a common-law marriage. After arriving in Los Angeles in 1903, she had hired a lawyer and obtained a divorce from Rodríguez. Her lawyer had assured her that the common-law relationship with John Van Order offered all the rights and privileges of a legal marriage for her and her children. In the months since their return from Los Angeles, John had been wont to come and go in a desultory fashion, almost as a stranger. Beyond being her interpreter, caring for her physical needs, and fathering her children, he had little in common with her. He meant well, but was utterly devoid of sensitivity. Never had two people been less attuned to one another. The person in her immediate family who would miss her least when she was gone would be John Van Order.

Reaching into the distant past, Teresita pieced together memories of her mother, Cayetana. She remembered the Indian woman as a sweet, gentle person, misused and mistreated. Teresita had made an effort to keep in touch with her mother, but Cayetana could neither read nor write and was seldom around those who could. A compelling urge to see her mother once more possessed Teresita, and she sent money for train fare to her last known address. Unknown to her daughter, Cayetana was then in Nogales, Sonora.

In her reflections, Teresita thought very little about death. It held no terror for her. Countless times she had witnessed it as the greatest of blessings. Now that it was her turn, the prospect seemed no more frightening than that of a pleasant journey to unknown places.

During the latter part of the day, callers often came to see Teresita. One of these was Mrs. Rosencrans, the banker's wife, accompanied by the son Teresita had cured some five years before. He was a big, healthy boy now, and only dimly remembered in the gaunt figure before him the beautiful girl who had made him well. Mrs. Rosencrans commented on how much taller, thinner and more fragile Teresita appeared since her return. Teresita smiled wanly and inquired after the boy's health. Before leaving, Mrs. Rosencrans offered to send her carriage and driver to take Teresita any place she wished to go. At this suggestion, some of the color returned to Teresita's face and her eyes brightened.

"Thank you. There is a place I would like to go. The Shannon Hill Cemetery. I want to visit my father's grave."

"Very well. When?"

"Tomorrow? Late in the afternoon?"

So it was arranged. Such a visit was something Teresita had longed to make ever since her return, but not one of Don Tomás's horses or carriages remained. She was told that at the time of the property settlement all the horses and vehicles had been taken away by Buenaventura, as administrator of the estate.

Next day she absent-mindedly tended her flowers while her thoughts returned to her father. Soon she forgot the flowers entirely and sat in a small rocker, gazing out of the window, absorbed in complete reverie. Memories did not come in chronological sequences, but darted about here and there.

She recalled the evening Don Tomás came home after she first arrived at Cabora: how he had sat at the table, looking from her to Gabriela and back to her. That was the time she discovered that unlike most men, he had a poetic aspect that he usually kept well hidden. Next she remembered the moment at the well at Santana when she was still only a ragged village urchin; how Don Tomás had stopped and gazed at her as he sat on his magnificent horse. And a time during the exodus when, as she was helping to drive the goats, he had dashed by her, but then had turned in his saddle to look back at her. And there was the day at Cabora when Captain Enríquez came to arrest her. Her father and her four brothers had placed themselves between her and a whole company of federal soldiers. She knew they would have sacrificed themselves to the last man before they would have given up. Memory followed memory. She recalled her last glimpse of her father at the depot, standing apart and alone, the look on his face one of profound hurt.

What had she done to her father, she asked herself. She had changed his whole way of life. He had objected, and fought to avert the change, but had in the end put her and her interests above every other consideration: his family, his ranches, everything else that he loved. Because of her, he had even been exiled from his native land.

Tears welled in her eyes. She had wrought all these ruinous alterations in his life. Why had he allowed her to do so? Slowly she realized the very special place she had occupied in her father's affection, one shared by no other woman, unless it was his mother, Apolonaria. His love for Teresita, fiercely paternalistic, had set her in a category apart. Vaguely she sensed that perhaps she had filled a special spiritual need. She berated herself for being absent when he needed her most, at the time of his last illness. Her thoughts were interrupted when Mariana came bustling in to bring her a cup of tea.

That afternoon the weather changed for the worse. The sky was overcast with billowy, threatening clouds. Mrs. Rosencrans's driver arrived and asked if Santa Teresa still wished to be taken to the cemetery.

"Indeed I do," she answered; she was dressed and waiting. "This is just the kind of afternoon I was hoping for."

The rain fell as the carriage climbed the long, steep grade up Shannon Hill. Showers pelted the road before and behind the carriage, but not the conveyance itself. At length they reached the summit and entered the cemetery.

"Will you drive on and come for me in an hour? I would like to be alone," she told the driver.

Slowly, because of her shortness of breath, she began searching the area where she had been told Don Tomás was buried. She found the grave beneath a small wooden headboard bearing his name and the dates of his birth and death. Lowering herself

J. CISNEROS

onto a nearby rock, she gazed at the low mound of earth, which four years of rain, snow and wind had not succeeded in leveling. She tried to envision how he must look down there, just four or five feet below the surface—his features, his mustache, his eyes and hair. The picture would not emerge clearly. Instead she saw a vigorous man at the peak of his strength, guiding her around the ranch and explaining the irrigation system at Cabora. Try as she might she could not imagine her father dead. Memory followed memory as the clouds darkened. She was jarred from her reveries by a brilliant flash of lightning immediately followed by a clash of thunder. Drawing her cloak more tightly about her, she looked up and watched the dark, swelling clouds that now filled the sky. Rain seemed to be falling everywhere except upon the boulder on which she rested. Presently a shaft of light broke through the clouds, enveloping the cemetery in a pale, coppery light. The turmoil of clouds continued, changing shapes and positions rapidly—great, billowy masses lying close to the earth. Suddenly the mountain peaks on every side burst into view, reflecting a golden luminosity, while the valleys below remained dark and unfathomable.

"There is where my father is!" she thought, lifting her eyes to the heights. "He is not here." She rose and slowly turned, looking at the mountain crests rising about her in every direction. Her ecstasy grew as she gazed; her soul seemed to soar. The unearthly sensation was one she had experienced before, on rare occasions.

As the clouds were receding in the valleys, her gaze returned to the little mound, and then swept around the cemetery and its frame of mountains.

"Papá," she whispered, "We have the most beautiful resting place in the world. We could never find one more lovely."

She heard the driver call from the gate. As she walked away from the grave, she paused and looked back, as if to say, "I will return."

Descending Shannon Hill in the carriage, she slumped in

the back seat. Her spirit still soared, but her strength was depleted.

The next day, physically weakened and emotionally drained, she remained in bed until late afternoon. Then, with much effort, she rose and stood gripping the headboard of the bed, steadying herself. The trip to the cemetery had drawn upon her last reserves of strength. Leaning heavily on Mariana she made her way slowly to the Flower Room, where she sat gazing at her flowers and talking very little.

Next day there was no change. The family still did not realize the seriousness of her condition. Soon, they thought, she would begin to mend. In the afternoon Dr. Burtch called, and saw that she was wasting away rapidly. When they were alone, he stood gravely shaking his head. She understood what he meant, and gave a smile of fleeting sweetness. "I know. It will not be long now."

"I think we should tell them," the doctor replied urgently.

"No. It will only make them sad, and there is nothing they can do."

Teresita then outlined her wishes for the funeral arrangements, and requested that he take charge. He was the only person, she thought, who would understand her desires.

Two days later Cayetana arrived. It was for her coming, it seemed to Dr. Burtch, that Teresita had made the supreme effort to remain conscious. She drew upon her last energies to converse with her mother.

The next day she lay listless in bed until the afternoon, when she asked Mariana to help her to the Flower Room. Mariana and Cayetana, one on either side, all but carried her in and propped her against the pillows in a rocking chair. She asked that Mariana, Cayetana and her half-sister Anita have tea with her. The tea was prepared, and Teresita sipped a little of hers. With forced animation, she appeared almost gay, as she related an amusing story of her childhood with her mother. The women dared to hope that a turn for the better had occurred.

"I think I will now take a little rest," Teresita said to them.

The women helped her back to bed. Mariana arranged the pillows so that her head and shoulders were elevated. As they stood there watching, Teresita slipped away peacefully with the trace of a smile on her lips.

Dr. Burtch's records state that she died of consumption, but her family and the Latin-American population were convinced that she had worn out her spirit in the service of her people.

The funeral went off as she had instructed. Her frail body lay in state in the Flower Room while practically everyone in Clifton filed by to pay their last respects, with tears. No priest officiated, but musicians had been brought. As the body was taken from the house, they played "La Golondrina," the farewell song of Mexico. The funeral procession ascending Shannon Hill was the longest in the history of Clifton. Hundreds of mourners stood with bowed, bared heads as Teresita's body was buried beside that of Don Tomás.

In the funeral record of the Lewallen Mortuary, Clifton, Arizona, appears the following entry:

January 11, 1906
Santa Teresa
Age: 33 years
Place of death: Clifton
Time: January 11, 1906
Cause: Consumption
Doctor: L. A. Burtch
Funeral: From residence
Time: 3:00 P.M., January 13, 1906
Buried: Catholic Cemetery

Epilogue

THE SEARCH for Teresita led me, at one point, to the place where she was born. Road maps of northern Sinaloa were at the time practically nonexistent, but we knew that the Rancho de Santana was near Ocoroni, and could be reached by a dirt road winding across an arid and desolate expanse.

The town was small, old and weather-beaten. My wife and I had no trouble locating relatives of Don Tomás, surnamed Ortiz and Conobbio. They were living in what was left of the Ortiz home, which had once belonged to Don Tomás's mother. Without an interpreter communication was difficult, but we made them understand that we wished to see the place where Teresita was born. Curiosity turned to animated interest. The Ortiz relatives explained how we could get to the Santana Ranch. A country road led to it three miles west. The appearance of the ranch was as if we had arrived there a hundred years before, with the exception of an old car and a pickup truck very much the worse for wear. Everything else about the place appeared little changed since the time when Don Tomás and Doña Loreto had lived there in the 1870s. A short distance to the west we found the village called Protrero, where Teresita had lived in the ramada of her scolding aunt. The ramadas had been replaced over the years, but the sizes, shapes and furnishings had not been altered. There was no alignment or pattern to their positions; they were simply scattered here and there—some twenty-five to thirty of them. This meant that many families lived on the ranch and drew their sustenance from it.

The arrival of our camper in a cloud of dust created a sensation in the village. A hundred pairs of eyes were regarding us as we stopped in front of what we took to be the *patrón's* house. We had been told in Ocoroni that his name was José Angel Conobbio, a great-nephew of Don Tomás. We were scarcely out of the camper when we saw him coming to meet us. A man in his forties, of average height, slightly rotund, he wore flannel trousers with a freshly washed and ironed white shirt, open at the collar, and a cattleman's type panama hat. He had a clipped mustache, his complacent face was smooth, and his small hands were soft. His well-made shoes were of good leather. From the house where the old pickup was parked the *mayordomo* appeared. Lean and sinewy, with calloused hands, he stood a head shorter than the *patrón.* His tanned face with deep character lines radiated animation. His apparel consisted of a faded khaki shirt and trousers, a straw hat, the kind that costs about three pesos in a market, and rough, cowhide boots.

The *patrón*, with the politeness of upper-class Mexicans, introduced himself and then the *mayordomo*, Celso Léon. After this José Angel Conobbio seemed to defer to Celso. In the meanwhile several curious vaqueros strolled over from the ramadas. We explained that we were writing a book about Teresita and had come to see her birthplace. "Teresita" was a magic word. The faces of all within hearing distance lighted up. Celso beamed. Even the passive expression of Angel Conobbio seemed to indicate pleasure. Word spread rapidly, and soon we were surrounded by practically every person in the village and the houses, all straining to hear what we had to say. It was Celso who responded, explaining that the exact spot was on the Santana Arroyo about a half mile to the north. There was no problem in driving there.

We would go at once. It was obvious that Celso was the one who ran the ranch. He suggested that Angel ride with us, and he would come in the pickup. He cranked it up, with a loud back-fire or two, and got it running. The vaqueros and their women and children piled in and on it, twenty-five or thirty of them. We waited for Celso to take the lead. Then behind us came everyone else in the village, walking.

The arroyo was a valley with no precipitous banks. It was covered with what appeared to be an impenetrable growth of bushes and stalky weeds, all higher than a tall man's head. We stopped the camper and got out. With Celso and Angel leading, we pushed our way through the brush along an obscure foot trail. The vaqueros and their families followed us.

Presently we came to a clearing in the brush. In the center stood a large cross planted firmly in the ground. It was no ordinary cross, but was carefully hewn from ironwood. Celso and Angel approached it, knelt, removed their hats, which they held over their hearts with their left hands, and crossed themselves with their right hands. We stood back and observed, while all the others did the same. The silent reverence was impressive.

After making their obeisances, the people formed a circle at the periphery of the clearing, about fifty feet in diameter. Celso explained that the ramada where Cayetana lived had stood in the center of the clearing, and that the cross marked the spot where she gave birth to Teresita, on a split carrizo mat, at the break of day October 15, 1873.

Furthermore, he said, Teresita's spirit returned to Santana and to this spot on every third day. He added, "This is the day. Do you not feel it?" The veneration of the people was so intense that it created a magnetic atmosphere that seemed to fill the area. The spell was contagious. We felt it—an exhilaration one seldom experiences—and it stiffened the hair on our necks. Here on this spot of ground, which we could touch with our hands, this extraordinary woman had been born, close to the earth and to her people.

Celso, like an officiating priest, let it be known that the silent service was over.

Then we noticed something that we had not been aware of before. All around the cross were tiny graves with small crosses. The mounds were well kept, some of them surrounded by low masonry walls. We asked Celso about them.

"This is called '*El Campo de los Angelitos*,' the field of the little angels," he said. "Children who die in infancy are buried here, where La Santa was born."

Appendix

Tomochic

THE WANTON DESTRUCTION of the mountain village of Tomochic in 1892 was to the Mexican Revolution what the Alamo in 1836 was to the Texas Revolution, a tragic symbol of a people rebelling against a despotic government.

In 1965 one of my former Texas Tech University history students, J. Merrill Kayser, read my first draft describing the Battle of Tomochic and developed a yearning to see the place. He and his wife, Dorothy, were both licensed pilots. Flying down in a small single-engine plane, they got to Tomochic but were unable to land. What they saw only stimulated Kayser's determination to try again in June 1966—this time over land. Later, I recorded on tape his account of the two trips.

"You recall, Dr. Holden, it was thirteen years ago. You had been working on the Saint of Cabora and I read your chapter on the Battle of Tomochic. For some reason I got an irresistible feeling that I had to make a pilgrimage to the place where Cruz Chávez and his band died to the last thirteen-year-old boy shouting "Viva la Santa de Cabora." There is something about the Sierra Madres in Chihuahua that draws adventurers such as me to them: the stories, the people, the gold and silver, and the wild life. Hidden in them are the Tarahumara Indians and beyond them, the Mayos and the Yaquis. I wanted to go to Tomochic, and suddenly I *had* to go to Tomochic. It was in November 1965, the month in which the tragic thing in the high sierras happened seventy-three years before. Dorothy and I decided to saddle up a little 115-horsepower, air-cooled airplane and fly to Juárez on a Friday after we finished the day at school [both were teachers in the Snyder Public Schools]. The next morning we had to file a flight plan. Most maps do not even have Tomochic on them, but the U.S. Aviation Authority did have maps of the Tomochic area. From talking with you I knew fairly well where the village was. So I drew a circle on the map and said I wanted to go there. We spent the night in Chihuahua City. Next morning I had to explain to the airport authority where I was going. I said, "Into the sierras." He said, "Cañon del Cobre?" I said, "No, not there. To Tomochic." He did not know what I was talking about. So I said, "I will not land there, but will return here." He thought we were crazy, but two less gringos would make little difference. So we filled up with gasoline and took off.

"Tomochic is about one hundred and thirty miles almost due west of Chihuahua City, which has a 4,400-foot elevation. We had to go up another six thousand feet to get over the intervening mountain ridges, so we started climbing from the outset. After we had gone half the distance we were over the most chewed-up land I have ever seen. A crow could not land down there without breaking a leg.

"That was when I began to get tense. In case of engine trouble there was no place to go. When our landmarks began to show up, it was evident Tomochic was behind the highest peak ahead of us. So we had to veer to the right hoping to intercept the Tomochic River, which flows north and joins the Yaqui River. If we could recognize the Tomochic stream we could fly up its valley until we came to the village. Below us the land became more hostile for aircraft, with ravines, scars, escarpments, giant boulders all mixed up. Suddenly I noticed the ground was coming up at us, and we were still climbing all the little plane could stand. I had to make a big circle and gain another couple of thousand feet. The altimeter registered ten thousand feet, and the contours on the map showed 9,500 feet. We had reached the altitude limit the little plane could make. I was in almost a state of paralytic tenseness as we topped the ridge, and to my enormous relief there was the Tomochic River. At least we hoped it was.

"Easing up on the throttle and heading up the valley, in a few minutes I knew we were right. The valley opened up a mile or so wide for a distance of three or four miles. I recognized the Hill of the Medrano rising from the floor of the valley, and just beyond and to the left like a big bullfrog was what I took to be the Hill of the Cave. We began a descent while circling the valley. Coming back from the south, the mouth of the cave was plainly visible. Now I was sure this was the place! I had the same sensation I later had when I stood on the Acropolis and looked at the Parthenon. In awe, the hair on my head stood on end. Right below us was where it all happened. We were there. We recognized the cemetery. There was the new church alongside the mound of stones that was the old church where the women and children had been cremated. We circled, dropping down until just above the tops of the present-day houses, fifteen or twenty of them. Two or three fences with posts made of peeled pine crossed the valley enclosing a corn field. We came down to where the wheels of the plane just cleared the fences, looking for a place to land and take off. The smoke from the houses was going straight up, and the feel of the plane told me we would never be able to take off if we landed, until there was an updraft of air currents in the valley, which might not occur for several days. So I pulled the plane up to about fifty feet and we made two or three other circles while Dorothy shot pictures from the cockpit. Then I opened the throttle wide to get altitude, but the lift was scarcely perceptible. It was the time of day when there was a down draft in the bowl-like valley.

We still had a half tank of gasoline, and I knew we could make it back, so we made one more circle to get a final overall view of the village, and identify all the points. The village was

L-shaped with houses on either side of the road. Once over the ridge it was downhill all the way to Chihuahua City, where we spent the night, and home next day.

"We had been to Tomochic, but our pictures were not very good. I was not satisfied. There was some compensation for having first seen the layout from above. I knew I had to go back, walk in the tracks used by Cruz Chávez and his bearded men, feel the soil in my hands and talk to the people. I wanted to know what their attitude was toward the people who perished there three-quarters of a century before. In June the following summer, 1966, we tried it again, this time over land. Our plan was to go by car to Chihuahua City where Dorothy would stay with a school-teacher friend. I would take the Oldsmobile and drive as close as I could to Tomochic, either to Guerrero or some other town. Then I would find transportation; ride a horse, or walk if necessary. I assembled a backpack so as to be ready for any eventuality.

"All went as planned, and just out of Chihuahua City I picked up a hitch-hiker going to the next village. I asked him about Tomochic, and he knew nothing. Farther along I got another hitch-hiker. When I inquired about Tomochic, he said, 'Oh, you mean Temosachi. Yes, I know about it.' I explained it was Tomochic I wanted, not Temosachi. He did not know. The third hiker I found did know. I asked if there was a road, and he said there was a road. I asked how long had the road been made, how many years? He said, 'No years.' 'How many weeks?' 'One.' I concluded they had just got a bulldozer through to the Tomochic valley. I asked if he would go with me as a guide. He could not go because he was due at a ranch close by. I drove on to Guerrero alone.

"I parked on the city square. It does not matter where you stop in the rural towns in Mexico. In thirty minutes everybody in town will know who you are and what you are there for. Before I could get out of the car a young fellow came over and asked if he could help me. I asked about the road to Tomochic.

He said there was a road, but only a truck with a high center could make the trip. The news spread fast. In a few minutes another boy came running to tell me there was a man who had a truck who was going to take a load of hay to Tomochic. The man was out of town, but would be back in the late afternoon. This sounded like a godsend. Later in the afternoon a boy came running from the town to tell me the hay hauler was back at his house. A half-dozen boys offered to show me the way. I told them all to pile in and we went swooping into town well guided and well guarded. The man was working on his truck under the shade of a tree. The truck was at least twenty years old and had no doubt traveled two hundred thousand miles. It was owned by two middle-aged brothers. They were going to Tomochic as soon as they could finish with the truck and load the hay. They agreed to take me there and back for two hundred pesos (twenty-five dollars). I could leave the car at their place and their families would guard it.

"I put my pack in the truck and we took off about an hour before sunset. From time to time there would be Indians getting on or off the load of hay. We crossed the river three or four times at low water fords. This river flowed south, then east and joined the Conchos, which in turn joined the Rio Grande at Presidio. We went west about six miles and then turned south toward Tomochic. The road was fairly good to Agua Fria. I commented on the name, and the driver said, 'No agua. Mucha fria.' (No water, much cold.) Beyond there the road had been bladed out just the width of a truck. It wound back and forth over ridges and ravines. The further we went the higher the ridges and deeper the ravines. The latter were narrow and deep. The road builders had bridged them by putting four or five logs across. On these, crosswise, were thick, rough-sawed boards, and on these dirt. The bridges were about eight to nine feet wide. It was a matter of hitting them dead center. A variation of a foot either way might be disastrous. The lights on the truck were not very good. The only consolation was that the driver was sober.

"About 3:30 the driver pulled off on a slope, stopped the motor and said, 'Let's get some rest.' I put on everything I had with me and rolled up in two blankets and was still cold. This was in June. I do not know how the Mexicans managed. Apparently they had nothing to cover themselves with.

"When the sun came up I awoke and they were getting ready to go. We were on the rim above Tomochic. I looked down upon it with the same thrill I had experienced in the airplane. I forgot how tired I was. We got in the truck and coasted down into the village. Coming from the north we passed the cemetery, then came to the little buildings on either side of the road. Some were made of logs and some of sawed lumber, all since 1900. About three hundred yards and across a small arroyo was the new church. We stopped the truck on a proper incline on the road where the houses were.

"The brothers insisted on taking me immediately to the church. Probably they had in mind that we should give thanks for not having missed a bridge during the night. I kinda felt that way too. So I crossed myself when we entered. One of them asked me if I were a Catholic. I said no, I was a Methodist, but I had a lot of Catholic friends. This pleased them. It was a nice, clean Mexican church with a belfry, and resembled the descriptions of the old church.

"I was more interested in the mound of the old church, which was alongside the new one, and I had a strong desire to begin digging. The men went back to the truck. We had agreed to meet in the late afternoon. I found a vantage point and stood with closed eyes, imagining the old church reconstructed, filled with women and children. Men in the belfry keeping a Mexican army at bay with their Winchesters. Then the burning of the church, women dragging children barefoot through flames, clothing afire, screaming, crying, dying. I opened my eyes, and there was the mound. Again I had that hallowed feeling. Then I turned and climbed up to the cave in the Hill of the Cave just east of the church. The cave was some fifty feet wide, twenty-five feet high at its entrance and extended back into the hill about forty feet. There was no evidence that the fill on the floor had ever been excavated. It could contain prehistoric artifacts. I did not go to the top of the hill, which had cost General Rangel several hundred men to take it from a handful of determined Tomochitecos.

"From the floor of the cave I was about on the same level as the top of the Hill of the Medrano on the opposite side of the valley. There General Rangel had placed his little cannon and pounded the church and the House of Cruz for days with little effect. I went back by the church and passed the school: one room, one teacher, and fifteen to twenty children. I wanted to go in and talk with them, but my time was limited. I went back to the houses along the road. Each one had a privy behind it. I did not check on where the water came from, probably shallow wells. In the days of Cruz Chávez it was from the river. The federal government in recent times has reached out to these faraway places and is trying to do something for the common people.

"I started to the Hill of the Medrano. It is about three hundred feet from the valley level to the crest and rather steep with very little vegetation. I had to go back and forth to make the climb. On top, one has a superb view of the village. In fact, it was from this point General Rangel observed the battle that lasted nine days. I picked up an empty brass shell of a bullet. It could have been one used in the attack. I stood for some time reconstructing the plan of battle, as I remembered it from the manuscript. The Tomochic River flows on the west side of the hill. I could see how it was possible for Colonel Torres, with his six hundred troops from Piños Altos, to unite his contingent with that of General Rangel by going behind the hill.

"Back in the village I talked with several local people. About twelve families lived there, some twenty-five adults and forty to sixty children. In all, not over eighty people, compared to nearly four hundred in 1892. Few, if any, of the present population are descendants of those who lived there before the destruction of the original town. The current inhabitants have a fierce pride in Cruz Chávez and his martyred men. The overall attitude toward the complete annihilation of the male population and many women and children is comparable in every way to that of the Daughters of the Texas Revolution concerning the destruction of the Alamo. I believe that with a half-dozen Winchesters and a carton of shells I could have started a little revolution then and there. It was mid-afternoon, and my hay haulers were waiting. With three hours of sleep during the previous thirty-six, suddenly I felt tired and spent, and was ready to leave. However, as the old truck labored and strained on the long climb to the rim of the valley, I experienced a feeling of exaltation. I had been to Tomochic."

An Interview with Teresita

The Examiner, San Francisco: Friday Morning, July 27, 1900

SANTA TERESA, CELEBRATED MEXICAN HEALER, WHOSE POWERS AWE WARLIKE YAQUIS IN SONORA, COMES TO RESTORE SAN JOSE BOY TO HEALTH

By Helen Dare

San Jose, July 26.—Santa Teresa is in California.

That self-same Santa Teresa who has been worshiped as a guide from heaven by the Indians of Mexico on our southern border; who has been credited with miraculous healing powers; who was thrown into prison in Mexico charged with causing an uprising of the Yaqui Indians; who was banished from Mexico for the same reason; who has been the cause of uprising and bloodshed wherever she has appeared in Mexican towns or villages, and excited the fears of the authorities by the enthusiastic following her presence provided; who has gone about healing by the laying on of hands—as believers claim—until her fame has so spread that her presence in any place turns that place into a camp of sufferers flocked to see her; who was, it is claimed, the real cause of a bloody attack on the custom-house at Nogales, Sonora, Mexico, some four years ago, by a religiously crazed band of Pima Indians, Mexican peons, Yaquis and Mestizos; who only last month was the occasion of another sensation in Arizona, when she was married on one day to a Mexican there, who on the next day went mad and attempted to shoot her—that self-same Santa Teresa is now in California.

She arrived at noon to-day.

She is in a modest, cosy, commonplace, white-painted cottage at 235 North Seventh Street, San Jose—an ordinary, modern, white-painted, frame cottage, with very modern, bright Brussels carpets on the floors, an electric button at the door and an electric car buzzing by half a block away—is this strange Jeanne d'Arc of the Indians; a saint in a shirt-waist and a sailor hat.

Santa Teresa—whose name as she writes it is Teresa Urrea —has been famed for twelve years in Mexico, in New Mexico, in Arizona and Texas, as a healer and a being endowed with supernatural powers. She was charged with having caused an uprising of the Yaquis and was imprisoned in Guaymas in 1891. She was banished, and the decree caused the Tomochic Indians to go on the warpath.

The Governor of Sonora, as the quickest way to bring about peace, allowed her to return, which she did in 1893, the Indians and ignorant Mexicans making a great rejoicing over her. They crowded to Cabora, where she was, in great numbers, bringing their sick and crippled, filling the town and dotting the mountain sides. Their numbers and enthusiasm so alarmed the Governor that she was warned out of the country again. Before she left, it was said that sixty Yaqui braves rode up to her door and presented her with several thousand dollars worth of gold dust and nuggets.

Next she was using her healing powers in Presidio del Norte, Mexico, where she was again arrested, a fight ensuing between her followers and the authorities, in which one man was killed. Since then she has lived in this country in Nogales, Ariz., in El Paso, Texas, and in Clifton, Ariz., creating a furor wherever she has been.

And this strange woman, who has incited fanatic worship, insurrection and persecution, who has been knelt to, fought over, feared and banished, I found in the bright little parlor of this white-painted cottage in San Jose.

She came to meet me with a soft, swift, gliding step, a

slender out-stretched hand, a soft-spoken Spanish greeting—a tall, slender, flat-chested, fragile, dark-skinned young woman of distinctly Spanish-Mexican type with great, beautiful, black-fringed, shining brown eyes and a grave sweet smile.

The weariness and dust of travel was still on her. She wore a green silk bodice and a blue cloth skirt made in the mode—as nearly as they approach it in Clifton, Arizona. She had little gold knob earrings in her ears, a big gold pin through her thick rope of black hair coiled loosely and carelessly with no obvious vanity at the back of her head, and the heavy wedding ring on her hand the only other ornament.

She sat herself down beside me with her long slender hands together on her knees with the perfect ease of perfect unself-consciousness.

Santa Teresa speaks only Spanish, and Mrs. A. C. Fessler, whose guest she is and whose daughter's little child they believe she saved from death, interpreted for me the first full story of her strange life that Santa Teresa has told to be printed. Santa Teresa's thoughts take often the form of epigram, and one of her epigrams is—"Truth is everything; of truth I have no fear; in truth I see no shame." Then she said:

"I am twenty-eight years old. I was born in Sinaloa, Mexico. My mother was a very poor Mexican girl. Her name was Cayetana Chavez. My father was well-to-do. His name is Tomás Urrea. I am not a legitimate child. My mother was only fourteen when I was born. My father has eighteen children and my mother four, and not one of them is my own brother or sister. I went to school when I was nine years old, but I did not want to study; but later I felt I wanted to know how to read, and I learned my alphabet from a very, very old lady. My writing came to me of itself. I wanted to write, and I wrote, but how I learned I don't know, for I was not taught. On the floor of my mother's house I first wrote with my little finger in the dust.

"When I was sixteen my father sent for me to come into his home. I went to his hacienda in Cabora. It was adobe, the walls inside white and painted part of the way up as they paint them in Sonora. There for three months and eighteen days I was in a trance. I know nothing of what I did in that time. They tell me, those who saw, that I could move about but that they had to feed me; that I talked strange things about God and religion, and that the people came to me from all the country around, and if they were sick and crippled and I put my hands on them they got well. Of this I remembered nothing, but when I came to myself I saw they were well.

"Then when I could remember again, after those three months and eighteen days, I felt a change in me. I could still if I touched people or rubbed them make them well. I felt in me only the wish to do good in the world. I spoke much to the people about God—not about the church, or to tell them to go to church, but about God. I told them what I believe: that God is the spirit of love; that we who are in the world must love one another and live in peace; otherwise we offend God. When I offend I say to the one whom I have pained: 'Sister or brother, I have offended you. I ask forgiveness.'

"When I cured people they began to call me Santa Teresa. I didn't like it at first, but now I am used to it.

"Some said I was a saint, and some said there was an evil spirit in me. Some have come to examine and said it was in the blood or the nerves; but I feel it is given me from God. I believe God has placed me here as one of his instruments to do good.

"The power to do good makes me happy and grateful. I have no wish to be paid. I do not care for fine things or fine houses or money. I will refuse no one to help him. Sometimes I know people come to me because they have curiosity and no faith in me. If they are sick I try to cure them. I try not to have the same feeling against them that they have against me. Sometimes I feel this power that is in me come back when I send it to them, but I try again.

"When sick people come to me sometimes I can see where

they are sick just as if I was looking through a window. Sometimes I cannot.

"When I cure with my hands I do like this," and she took my hands in hers—hands of singular slenderness and fineness, cool, smooth, supple, firm, delicately made, charming to the touch—and placed her thumbs against mine, holding with a close, nervous grasp.

"Sometimes," she said, "I rub; sometimes I give also medicines or lotions that I make from herbs I gather. I pray, too, not with the lips, but I lift up my spirit to God for help to do his will on earth."

About her imprisonment in Mexico she says:

"I had nothing to do with the Yaqui revolution. They were fighting always to keep their land. Because the people followed me I was put in prison in Guaymas when I was eighteen years old—not in the jail, but in a private place opening on a cattle corral, where the mosquitoes ate me. The people gathered around me there and wanted to take me out, so the Government told my brother-in-law to take me out of the country. I have cured the Indians and they love me for it, but I do not tell them to make revolutions.

"I have cured many people—when I was in El Paso, Texas, sometimes I cured two hundred in a day."

"And you were happy?" I asked.

"Si, Señora," she said, "happy and grateful—but not proud. Happy to do as Christ did."

About her marriage she spoke herself, with the same absence of self-consciousness, with the same straightforward simplicity she told the rest of her story.

"I was married," she said, "on the 22nd of June—last month —to Guadeloupe N. Rodrigues. He is Mexican. I had known him eight months. The next day after we were married he acted strangely; he tore up some things of mine, packed some of my clothes in a bundle, put it over his shoulder, and said to me,

'Come with me!' The people who saw him said for me not to go, but I followed him. He walked on the railroad track. I did not know where he wanted to go, but I would follow. Then he began to run. I ran, too. He had his gun and started to shoot. The people ran out and made me come back. Then they caught him. He was insane and they put him in jail. There is where he is now."

"You loved him?"

"Yes, that is why I married him."

"And you thought you ought to marry?"

"To marry, Señora, is one of God's laws. I did not disobey. He would not be displeased."

And now it is Santa Teresa's wish to go over the world healing. Not to have fine clothes, fine houses and fine living, but to have only, as she has always had, simple fare and simple raiment, and to go from place to place using the power she believes she has.

She was brought here from Clifton, Arizona, by Mrs. C. P. Rosencrans to heal her little, three-year-old child.

"My little boy, Alvin," says Mrs. Rosencrans, "was dying of cerebro-spinal meningitis two months ago. He was sick two weeks and then five doctors we called said there was no hope. He became blind, he couldn't move, and when his little hands were clenched so he couldn't open them, when he couldn't speak or move we at last asked Santa Teresa to come to him. She put a plaster on his back and rubbed him for half an hour and he could open his hands. She has been caring for him for six weeks and he can move and talk, he is fat again, and I believe," and the little mother's heart choked up into her throat, "that she will cure him and make him see again."

This is what the little blind boy's mother says.

From wherever Santa Teresa has been come tales—the tales that are always told of healers—of marvelous cures, from El Paso, Texas, where they wanted to build Santa Teresa a home and keep her, many tales with names of people she has cured, from Nogales, Arizona and Clifton. The Indians around Clifton are devoted to her, as are the Indians wherever she has been, and on the morning she left fifty of them came to say good-bye to her—got up at 3 in the morning to walk to Clifton and wept as she went away, because they fear she will not come back.

Whether Santa Teresa is a spiritual healer or not it is not given to me to know—nature has not endowed me with faith.

But Santa Teresa believes she is—devoutly, humbly, passionately believes she is. She doesn't pose; she doesn't persuade; she only answers questions in a straightforward, unhesitating way, never dodging, never resorting to subterfuge, never for a moment trying to hide anything or explain away anything.

The glance of her beautiful brown eyes is half sad and wholly intelligent, without any of the cunning or the sleepiness or the furtive watchfulness of the ordinary Mexican or Indian, and she has in her modest, fragile person and her quiet manner such a dignity, such earnestness and sincerity and gentleness and serenity that one cannot deny her respect, even when faith is unconvinced.

Notes to the Text

Introduction

p. xi. Only in recent years have Mexican historians, digging deeper into the social and economic causes of the Mexican Revolution of 1910 and 1920, listed Teresa Urrea's influence as an unpremeditated factor in starting the Revolution.

p. xiii. In the 1890s the Porfirio Díaz government expropriated Yaqui lands and gave them to wealthy Mexicans and Americans. Twenty years later, in the 1920s, the Obregón government built a dam on the Río Yaqui upstream in the foothills of the Sierra Madres and diverted the water to the fertile coastal plan south of the river. A vast and profitable irrigated region was the result, a boon to everyone except the Yaquis. This was one of the more recent of their grievances against the government.

Prologue

p. 3. This incident was described to the author by Henry Aguirre, March 25, 1962. A fuller account of Mendoza's visit to Cabora appears in Chapter 9.

Chapter 1

p. 7. Cayetana has been described by some writers as a Yaqui Indian. Aside from the fact that she was a mestizo several shades lighter than full-blooded Indians, the error is understandable. Her mother was a Tehueco. The Tehuecos and Yaquis, along with six other tribal groups living between the Fuerte and Yaqui rivers, spoke a common language, Cahita. The Yaquis, most warlike of all the Cahita groups, have loomed large in the troubled history of Mexico and have received virtually all the publicity. This accounts for the tendency to call anyone who speaks Cahita a Yaqui. For similar reasons, Teresita was later reputed to be part Yaqui. Other writers have referred to Cayetana as a Mayo Indian. This mistaken designation is probably attributable to the fact that Cabora was located midway between the Mayo and Yaqui rivers. Teresita's influence with the Mayos was also far greater than with any other Cahita-speaking group, including the Yaquis.

p. 10. We found Teresita's full name in the baptismal records of the Roman Catholic Church, Sinaloa Leyna.

p. 11. The source for the description of Teresita's childhood environment is Lauro Aguirre, *La Santa de Cabora* (El Paso, Texas, Texas, 1902), p. 5.

Chapter 2

p. 15. The information in this chapter is based largely on the recollections of Marcos Alvarado. To my knowledge, he is the only person living (at the time of my research) who participated in every phase of the events that follow. Alvarado was in his middle twenties in 1880 when Don Tomás moved his family and chattels; he was placed in charge of driving the livestock with help from several vaqueros.

p. 18. Mesquite has been a dominant factor in the primitive economy of the coastal plain of Sonora and Sinaloa. The trees grow large, tall and reasonably straight; something in the soil and arid climate agrees with them. Railroad ties of the Sud Pacifico from Guaymas to Mazatlán were later hewn from mesquite. It furnished the posts and cross timbers for the ramadas, posts for fences, and fuel for cooking and warmth. No other wood compares with it, and the aroma of its smoke is unmistakable—a pleasing, subtle, aromatic incense.

p. 19. The Mayo Indians are not related to the Mayas of Yucatan in any way, ethnologically, linguistically or geographically.

p. 25. Antonio Alvarado, a witness to the event, described to us the confrontation between Doña Loreto and her husband.

p. 26. Don Tomás's descendants in the third generation were rather tolerant of their grandfather's propensities. In 1962, Gustavo

Santini, whose mather, Juliana, was Doña Loreto's daughter, told us, "My grandfather was never happy in his marriage with my grandmother. He never loved her. It was a marriage of economic convenience arranged by their Uncle Miguel. Doña Loreto was timid and retiring—a very religious woman who considered sensual pleasure a sin. She was always afraid of my grandfather and could never stand up to him. She could never cope with him physically or psychologically."

Chapter 3

p. 27. Marcos and Antonio Alvarado could not remember precisely what happened to Cayetana, but both have advanced the opinion that she probably drifted off with some vaquero or passing mine worker.

p. 27. Years later, in a newspaper interview for *The Examiner,* San Francisco, July 27, 1900, Teresita was reported as saying, "I grew up in the lazy, ignorant way of Mexican children. I went to school, but did not like to study."

p. 28. There is a difference of opinion as to when Teresita came to Cabora. One Mexican historian, Mario Gill, stated that "she spent her childhood at Cabora." (*Episodios Mexicanos,* Mexico, 1960). This we know is in error. Lauro Aguirre, a civil engineer who surveyed the boundary line between Sinaloa and Sonora, was acquainted with Don Tomás before he moved from Sinaloa. He was a visitor to Cabora from time to time during the 1880s and later became an ardent supporter of Teresita. In 1896, while publishing *El Independiente,* an anti-Díaz newspaper in El Paso, Texas, he wrote and printed on his own press a book entitled *La Santa de Cabora* (1902). On page 5 he says: "The identity of Teresita's father was known only to her mother, her aunt and herself. [The identity of her father was probably better known to people on all the Urrea ranches than Don Lauro realized.] Because of the abhorrent life in her aunt's house, Teresita, when about fifteen years old, of her own volition, went to Don Tomás, identified herself and asked for his help. Don Tomás acknowledged his paternity and installed her at Cabora." This version agrees with a statement Teresita made to a newspaper reporter some fifteen years later in Saint Louis: "When I was fifteen my father sent for me and I went to his hacienda, called Cabora." This places her arrival at Cabora in 1888.

It is also likely that Don Tomás had kept his eye on Teresita when visiting the ranches over the years. He must have watched her growth through adolescence and was undoubtedly aware of her developing beauty and intelligence. At some point he must have determined that she was a daughter of whom he could be proud and made the decision to recognize her as his child and bring her to Cabora.

p. 30. We are indebted to Marcos Alvarado, who joined the group escorting Teresita to Cabora, for details of her arrival and reception at the Casa Grande, which he related to us some seventy years after the event.

p. 33. Apolonaria Urrea Guttiérez offered the sequel to Marcos Alvarado's story of Teresita's reception. At the time, she was almost the same age as Gabriela and Teresita. Although she was not present, she received a full account from Huila following the event.

Chapter 4

p. 37. Information concerning Teresita's life during the two years following her arrival at Cabora in 1888 is extremely scant. I was unable to unearth any written material pertaining to this period, and of the scores of persons I interviewed, only three had known Teresita during her early years at Cabora. Marcos Alvarado saw her only occasionally when he went to the Casa Grande to confer with Don Tomás regarding ranching activities. Antonio Alvarado, who saw her almost daily in Sinaloa and as long as she remained at Aquihuiquichi, seldom glimpsed her after she became a member of the family of the *patrón*. Apolonaria, her half-sister, visited Cabora from time to time, but the state of Apolonaria's health, when my wife and I talked to her in Hermosillo, did not permit us to tire her with questions. We were anxious to learn the details of Teresita's transformation from an unwanted child to the *patrón*'s cherished daughter. Only Apolonaria was able to describe at first hand the episodes and events recounted on pages 37 to 46.

p. 42. The trail of Lauro Aguirre was one of the most elusive encountered during the course of our research on Teresita. Our search began in 1962 when we went to El Paso, where Aguirre was known to have published *El Independiente* in 1896 and *El Progresista* in 1902. From these two newspapers José C. Valades had obtained much of the information for his articles in *La Opinión* in 1937. After two days of searching, we located a retired typesetter who had learned his trade along with one of Aguirre's sons, Enrique. Enrique Aguirre had moved to the West Coast, probably to Los Angeles, while still a young man in his twenties, and later changed his name to Henry.

Teresita

The Los Angeles telephone directory listed a number of people named Henry Aguirre or Enrique Aguirre. By a stroke of luck, my first call produced the very person we were seeking. Henry Aguirre, then in his seventies, remembered well his father's relationship with the Urrea household and readily agreed to talk to us. At our meeting he showed us a copy of Lauro's book, *La Santa de Cabora*, first published in 1896. Henry's volume, a 1902 reprint, was to our knowledge the only extant copy of the book. Because I was reluctant to borrow this valued document, Henry very kindly had a photostat copy of *La Santa de Cabora* made for us.

During our interview, we learned that Lauro Aguirre had been a graduate in engineering from the Military Academy in Mexico City, a school whose standards in the 1860s were higher and whose discipline was even more rigid than those of the University of Mexico. Henry considered his father the best-educated and most brilliant man he had ever known. Lauro had owned an extensive library containing the works of the outstanding philosophers from Plato to the writers of the nineteenth century, all of which he had read.

Henry was a small child when Teresita and Don Tomás were in El Paso in 1896, and he vaguely remembered seeing them, but he was too young at the time to understand why they were there or to be aware of his father's role in the Mexican Revolution. He did, however, recall that when he was older he heard his father tell many stories about his association with the Urrea family. After Teresita's death, Lauro often said that she had inherited her father's intellect, his retentive memory, and his capacity for mental growth.

p. 49. José C. Valades wrote of an instance in which Teresita transferred her power of strength to her friend Josefina Félix (*La Opinion*, February 28, 1937). A Señor Ontillon from Nuri, a very strong man, so it was said, challenged Teresita to a game of *vencidos*. She said, "No, thank you. I suggest you play with Josefina." Josefina hesitated, saying that she was no match for such a powerful man. But Teresita insisted, declaring, "I command you to do it." Josefina pressed her opponent's arm and, to her surprise, was able to force his arm down. Everyone present was astounded to see such a strong man beaten by a woman. The incident reported by Valades was also recounted to us by several unrelated persons who had been present during this extraordinary feat. Also, José Esquerres, the grandson of the friends of Don Tomás, had known Josefina and remembered some of the stories he had heard her tell, including the incident described here, which he told to W.C.H. in 1962.

p. 51. Up until the time of Teresita's seizure facts about her life are sparse, but from this time on they become more abundant. Of this crucial period in her life I have been able to collect enough information, from many and varied sources, to fill a stack of notebooks. Some of the data comes from persons who actually witnessed the events at Cabora. Other accounts are at second-hand, from those whose friends and relatives told them what they had seen and heard. The stories contain minor discrepancies and confusions of dates, but on the whole, the similarities far outweigh the differences.

Of four Mexican historians who have written about Teresita, no two agree on her age at the time of the seizure. Valades places her age at twelve years. José C. Chávez in *Peleandro en Tomochic* states that she was under twelve. Mario Gill offers a variable estimate in his *Episodios Mexicanos*, saying that the seizure occurred "at the age of puberty." In *La Santa de Cabora*, Lauro Aguirre states that she was eighteen. My own research indicates that she was probably seventeen years of age at the time of her illness. We know that Teresita was expelled from Mexico on July 3, 1892, and that she had practiced her mystical cures for over two years before that date. Since these cures did not begin until after her seizure, the time of her illness can be dated about the later part of 1889 or early 1890.

Three of the historians mentioned classified the symptoms of Teresita's seizure as epileptic, or caused by a disorder of the nervous system. Lauro Aguirre stated they were cataleptic, implying rigidity of the muscles. No record exists as to how the seizure began, whether suddenly with a convulsion or with a coma.

p. 51. José C. Valades, *La Opinión*, February 22, 1937. Valades bases his assertion on an interview with Josefina Félix in Baroyeca, circa 1931. Josefina was Teresita's closest friend and confidante at the time of the attack, and she probably knew more about Millán's infatuation than any other person then living.

p. 52. The account of the next fourteen days is based largely on my interview with Apolonaria Urrea Gutiérrez, April 4, 1957.

Chapter 6

p. 62. This incident is noteworthy. In all likelihood, Teresita herself was not aware of transmitting the sensation. Later, many patients testified to feeling this "body magnetism" when she touched them. Months afterward a skeptical newspaper reporter described the feeling as a weak electrical current. The sensation seemed to be something Teresita unconsciously transmitted while concentrating on her patients. This mysterious charge, for which no evidence exists prior to Teresita's seizure, was the result of a newly acquired attribute caused by the illness or of an innate power that had remained dormant until activated by the attack.

p. 64. *New York Journal*, March 3, 1901. This may well have been the first time Teresita was called Santa, but in view of the events that were to follow, hundreds—or even thousands—of grateful recipients of her ministrations accorded her the title of saint.

p. 66. Aguirre, *La Santa de Cabora,* Chapter IV. Eleven years after the seizure, in an interview with a reporter of the *San Francisco Examiner*, July 27, 1900, Teresita said: "For three months and eighteen days I was in a trance. I knew nothing of what I did during that time. They tell me, those who saw, that I could move about, but they had to feed me, that I talked strange things about God and religion, and that people came to me from all over the country around, and if they were sick or crippled, I put my hands on them and they got well. Of this I remember nothing, but when I came to myself, I saw they were well."

Chapter 7

p. 69. In 1962, seventy-three years after this episode occurred, I asked Antonio Alvarado how Teresita knew that he was coming posthaste to Cabora long before he arrived. He gave much the same cryptic explanation: "She could see you before you got there."

Accounts of Teresita's abilities to "see" people and events at great distances sound remarkably similar to contemporary reports of "out-of-body experiences." In such experiences, it is believed, an "astral body" separates itself from the person's physical presence, and thus becomes free to travel to other places and even to other times. The astral self, which can get back into the body at will, is able to witness scenes and events not visible to the person's physical body.

Out-of-body experiences, or OOBEs, (also called "astral projection") are often generated through near-death situations, like Teresita's seizure. Robert A. Monroe, in his *Journeys Out of the Body*, Doubleday, 1973, states, "The OOBE is frequently an accident, a spontaneous uninvited occurrence. Sometimes illness, injury, or emotional stress can trigger it. It is usually a profound experience that radically changes a person's perceptions of himself, his environment, and his concept of life and his concept of life and death."

Chapter 8

p. 83. As we pursued Teresita's traces in the Sinaloa region of her birth, we asked those who had known Teresita or were related to her if they thought Teresita was a saint. Without exception, the answer was the same as that of Apolonaria, her half-sister: "No, she married, didn't she?" There seems to be a widespread belief that sainthood for women is connected with virginity; that to be a saint a woman must be pure, fresh and unused. This rule apparently does not seem to apply to male saints, a differentiation that creates a double standard for sainthood!

p. 83. Aguirre, *La Santa de Cabora*, ch. VIII, IX.

The story of this confrontation was told to us by Henry Aguirre, March 26, 1962. On March 22, 1962 a legitimate grandson of Don Tomás, Angel Santini, related to us this same story. Curiously, Santini had never seen Lauro Aguirre and did not know he had written a book about Teresita. His version, remarkably similar to Aguirre's, had been handed down through the family. Henry and Angel were completely unknown to each other.

p. 84. Aguirre offered an interesting sequel to the dramatic conversion: "The next morning, after Don Tomás's confrontation with Teresita, two books were delivered to him by a messenger on horseback. An anonymous note accompanying the package said, 'Read these books and you will better understand the work your daughter is doing!' Don Tomás read the books avidly, and in them he found explanations of the 'miracles' his daughter was bringing about. After that he not only accepted her good works, but did all he could to assist her."

We have no knowledge of the titles of these books or their contents. As to the sender, he was probably Aguirre himself. In the tumultuous events of 1892, the books were lost. In view of the fact that Don Tomás was a realist and a materialist, the books must have given him a means of establishing that the events, which the illiterate and superstitious masses at Cabora considered "miracles," could be accounted for by natural laws. Whatever the books contained, they enabled Don Tomás to reconcile his own convictions with Teresita's phenomenal activities.

p. 85. Gill, *Episodios Mexicanos*, p. 12.

p. 86. Research has established conclusively that he did not capitalize on Teresita's powers to create a source of profit, as Mario Gill has intimated in his *Episodios Mexicanos*, p. 13.

Chapter 9

p. 87. Henry Aguirre to W. C. H., March 26, 1962.

It is to be remembered that this story is twice removed from the reporter who actually witnessed the events treated. However, it rings true in essence to the facts we have gathered from first-hand and second-hand sources. We have been unable to ascertain whether or not Mendoza's article was published. However, we can assume that its contents conformed to the oral version he gave Henry Aguirre some thirty years after the occurrences took place.

Chapter 10

p. 99. All these colorful peripheral activities, labeled "The Cabora Fair" by Mario Gill, are similar to the goings-on at many shrines and holy places. The same carnival atmosphere exists around the Shrine of the Virgin of Guadalupe near Mexico City. In the time of Christ, the hucksters and vendors, collectively called "money changers," not only operated around the temple, but even moved inside.

p. 102 Aguirre, *La Santa de Cabora*, p. 7.

p. 105. Psychoanalysts are now studying such trances as a type of psychic phenomenon, and, according to Dr. Everlyn Montgomery, have given it a name, "limbic level of the mind."

p. 107. In the last few decades of the nineteenth century, a large number of educated people developed an interest in spiritualism—not so much as a religion, but more as a fascinating parlor game. Groups were organized to hold regular seances, and mediums could be found in almost every community. Like modern-day followers of the occult, the participants communicated with departed spirits through the medium, who asked questions and received answers from a table tapping on the floor or from some disembodied voice.

p. 107. Valades, *La Opinión*, February 28, 1937. Unfortunately, none of the data recorded by scientific observers has come to light. This, together with the fact that no clinical records of Teresita's treatments were kept, makes it impossible today to evaluate the conclusions of doctors or scientists.

p. 114. The Yaquis were much more inclined to regard Teresita in a political context than were their neighbors, the Mayos. Apolonaria Gutiérrez told us that on one occasion while she was at Cabora she witnessed the arrival of a group of Yaquis bearing a banner on which was inscribed in crude red letters, "Teresa, La Reina de los Yaquis"— a title more political than mystical.

Chapter 12

p. 117. The order of events is substantiated by historian Francisco B. Alamada in *La Rebelión de Tomochic,* exhaustively researched from the War Records in Mexico City.

Chapter 13

p. 131. The account of what took place at Cabora on December 24, 1891, and during the several days following, has been put together in part from the memories of an eyewitness, Marcos Alvarado, and in part from the articles in *La Opinión* of José C. Valades, who interviewed a number of other witnesses still living in 1937.

p. 132. Conflicting accounts exist as to how many troops Captain Enríquez brought to Cabora. Almada, who bases his estimate on official army reports, says in his *Diccionario* (Chihuahua, Mexico, n.d., p. 666) that there were forty dragoons. However, one must take into account that army reports were often made by officers who took liberties with numbers in order to explain their failures or to make themselves look good. Lauro Aguirre, who obtained his information from Don Tomás, who in turn was informed by his sons, says that there were one hundred men in the contingent.

p. 133. Aguirre noted that Torres was a Díaz henchman who had once served as governor of Sonora, and whose brother, Luís, held that office at the time of Teresita's "arrest."

Chapter 14

p. 141. The number of soldiers in Otero's contingent was not given in the reports. Eight years later in an interview with a reporter for the *San Francisco Examiner* (July 29, 1900), Teresita was quoted as saying, "The Mexican Government sent five hundred soldiers to arrest one nineteen-year-old girl."

p. 141. The decision to expel Teresita from Mexico, made at the highest level of government, was not based on her religion, her extra-sensory powers, or her curing, but was made purely for political reasons: she allegedly had helped to instigate the rebellions at Navojoa and at Tomochic. Two respected Mexican historians have found no evidence of treason or political agitation in Teresa Urrea's actions. José Carlos Chávez in his *Peleandro en Tomochic* wrote: "Teresita did not participate in the planning of the insurrections at Tomochic and Navojoa" (p. 70). In *La Rebelión de Tomochic* (p. 78), Francisco R. Almada stated: "In two documents [later brought to light] by men who officially conducted investigations at the time, Don Tomás Dozal y Hermosilla and the judge appointed by General Marcos Carrillo, neither one nor the other contained any reference whatever to Teresita's having incited the rebellion at Tomochic."

p. 148. This Mexican girl, who had appeared so suddenly in their midst, was a challenge to American newspaper reporters. She was fresh and titillating news. For fourteen years thereafter she offered prime copy. Stories about her, appearing in the period from 1892 to 1896, were for the most part political and international in substance, and were published from time to time on front pages of leading newspapers across the country. After 1896 the accounts dealt more frequently with her curing and were treated in feature articles, often filling an entire page, accompanied by photographs, usually close-ups of her miraculous hands. A few of the feature writers were cynical, but the large majority were sympathetic, some exceedingly so. An example appears in the Appendix, page 209.

Chapter 15

p. 156. After the campaign was over and the destruction of Tomochic was heralded in Mexico City as a "great victory over the barbaric heretics," the statements of Lieutenant Colonel Ramírez, quoted in newspaper reports of the incident, revealed a sincere respect and admiration for the Tomochitecos. He also spoke of the treatment the prisoners received. Cruz Chávez came in person to bring him food and to doctor him. All the prisoners were given the same food as the other people of the village: two tortillas each morning and evening. When there was meat, it was shared with the prisoners. They were also permitted to attend the religious services held daily.

p. 165. José Carlos Chávez, *Paleandros en Tomochic* (Ciudad Juárez, 1957).

Castro's story was edited and published by Chávez. Castro was a retired general and an old man when he gave the account to Chávez in 1957.

p. 166. José Carlos Chávez, *Peleandro en Tomochic* (Ciudad Juárez, Chihuahua, 1957), p. 121.

p. 166. President Díaz continued to squelch isloated rebellions such as Tomochic, and to rule Mexico solely for the benefit of his rich Mexican friends and foreign investors, until 1910. Then simultaneous uprisings in the north, the south and the center drove him from power. He fled the country and lived out his life in Paris. For the next ten years Mexico was torn and ravaged by rival factions struggling for control, led by such contenders as Madero, Huerta, Villa, Zapata, Carranza, and Obregón. The only constructive achievement of this decade of devastation was the drafting of the Constitution of 1917, perhaps the most democratic on the American continent. However, it was not completely implemented until many years later. General Alvaro Obregón succeeded in restoring national order in 1920. Subsequently Mexico enjoyed the most stable and enlightened government of all the Latin American nations.

Chapter 16

p. 170. Valades, *La Opinión*, May 16, 1937.

p. 174. This version of the Rodríguez affair is accepted by contemporary descendants of the Urrea family. It is unanimously believed that this unfortunate episode is the only out-of-character incident in Teresita's entire career.

Chapter 17

p. 186. We are dependent upon the memory of that remarkable woman, Mariana Avendano, for an account of events that took place during the last months of Teresita's life. She watched and later recounted the events to Anita and Marieta Urrea who, late in life, told them to us. So close was the bond between Mariana and Teresita that the two of them could communicate without words. The remainder of this chapter is based on what Mariana saw, felt and sensed.

p. 189. After Doña Loreto died at Cabora, Tomás *hijo* came and operated the ranch until the government expropriated the part on the south side of the arroyo. The remainder of the property was later owned by a grandson of Don Tomás, Angel Santini.

Selected Bibliography

Aguirre, Lauro. *La Santa de Cabora.* El Paso: El Progresista, 1902.

Almada, Francisco R. *Diccionario.* Ciudad Chihuahua: privately printed, n.d.

Almada, Francisco R. *La Rebelión de Tomochic.* Ciudad Chihuahua: privately printed, 1938.

Chávez, José Carlos. *Peleando en Tomochic.* Ciudad Juarez: privately printed, 1957.

Frias, Heriberto. *Tomochic.* Mexico, D.F.: Editora Nacional, 1960.

Gill, Mario. *Episodios Mexicanos.* Mexico, D.F.: Aztec Press, Editorial Aztec, 1960.

Parke, Henry Bomford, *A History of Mexico.* Cambridge: Riverside Press, 1960.

Priestley, Herbert Ingram. *The Mexican Nation.* New York: Macmillan, 1930.

Villegas, Daniel Casio. *Historia Moderna de Mexico: Vida Economica.* Mexico, D.F.: Editorial Hermes, 1955.

Villegas, Daniel Casio. *Historia Moderna de Mexico: Vida Politica.* Mexico, D.F.: Editorial Hermes, 1955.

Villegas, Daniel Casio. *Historia Moderna de Mexico: Vida Social.* Mexico, D.F.: Editorial Hermes, 1955.

Designed by Beverly Baum

Composed in 11-point Linotype Fairfield with Garamond Italic display by the Maryland Linotype Composition Company, Baltimore, Maryland

Printed on 70-pound Mohawk Ticonderoga Text, laid finish, and bound in paper by The John D. Lucas Printing Company, Baltimore Maryland

Bound in Joanna Kennett cloth by The Delmar Company, Charlotte, North Carolina